Talking to Myself

Lukcia

Patricia

Sullivan

Talking to Myself

POEMS FROM A
Transgender Woman during Transition

Lukcia Patricia Sullivan

ARCHWAY
PUBLISHING

Archway Publishing books may be ordered through booksellers or by contacting:

Archway Publishing
1663 Liberty Drive
Bloomington, IN 47403
www.archwaypublishing.com
844-669-3957

Because of the dynamic nature of the Internet, any web addresses or links contained in this book may have changed since publication and may no longer be valid. The views expressed in this work are solely those of the author and do not necessarily reflect the views of the publisher, and the publisher hereby disclaims any responsibility for them.

Any people depicted in stock imagery provided by Getty Images are models, and such images are being used for illustrative purposes only.
Certain stock imagery © Getty Images.

Interior Image Credit: Autumn Tierney and Michael Hallahan

ISBN: 978-1-6657-5706-5 (sc)
ISBN: 978-1-6657-5745-4 (hc)
ISBN: 978-1-6657-5707-2 (e)

Library of Congress Control Number: 2024903624

Printed in the United States of America.

Archway Publishing rev. date: 08/15/2024

For my sister Debbie and for Audrey.
These two women held my heart in their
hands while I became a girl.

In great appreciation of
Christine N. McGinn; Doctor, Scientist, Astronaut

The staff of the Papillon Center
These loving women made me a girl

And

Jennifer Finney Boylan; American Author
Her novels comforted me during my transition

I'm saying goodbye to people's
perception of me and who I am;
I'm not saying goodbye to me, because
this has always been me.

—*Caitlyn Jenner,*
Olympian and media personality

Contents

Foreword xi

Preface..xiii

Introduction xvii

Victor Stabin: The Turtle Series xix

1	I Lost My Mother.. 1
2	I Really Like Being a Girl 3
3	Courage..4
4	I Never Got to Be a Girl Until Now 5
5	Decisions...8
6	Bernard vs. Lukcia: What Is a Brand-New Girl to Do? 9
7	I Always Wanted to Be a Girl 12
8	No Poem Tonight...14
9	The Private Nature of What I Do..........................17
10	A Girl Maybe..19
11	Another Transgender Woman 20
12	Talking to Lukcia..22
13	Totally Under Control 23
14	To My Psychologist 24
15	Alcoholism Recovery Camp..................................25
16	Hair 26
17	A Poem for Ranay 28
18	The Challenge of Taking So Long........................29
19	Tough Night 31

20	Feeling Like a Girl	32
21	I Want to Be a Girl	34
22	Coming True	35
23	End of Your Life	38
24	Thank You for Yesterday	41
25	Love	44
26	How Do I Change My Mind?	46
27	Girl	48
28	Lipstick	50
29	I Don't Want to be Tough Anymore	52
30	I Am Only Her, I Am Only She, I Am Only a Version of "He"	54
31	I Am So Glad I Am Finally a Girl or Looking Through the Eyes of He	57
32	I Think I Am Going to Be a Bitch	59
33	Transgender Pain	61
34	If You're Not Dead	64
35	Facial en Femme	66
36	To Be in Love	68
37	What I Can't Do	70
38	The Tuck	72
39	Are My Nipples Large Enough?	74
40	I Am So Broken	75
41	Point B	77
42	A Final Poem to Peter	79
43	Allow Me to Be	80
44	Born Again	82
45	Heart Broken	84
46	Slightly Drunk	85
47	A Girl, Calm and Withdrawn	87
48	I Thought I Would be Nervous	89
49	How Can I Not Write a Poem?	91
50	Don't Look Up, Don't Look Down, Don't Look Inside to See How You Really Feel	93

51 To Have a Chance to Be 95

52 In Fantasy, I Am Soon to be a Girl 96

53 I Am in So Much Pain.. 99

54 No Longer Young...101

55 If It's PTSD, Then Thank You; It Let Me Become a Girl 102

56 I Am OK... 105

57 I Talked with You Today 107

58 In Bed at Three...110

59 Proud of Me 112

60 Talking to Someone Other Than Me..................................114

61 A Hard Time Writing a Poem 116

62 Bernard...119

63 How to be Sad, How to be Glad, How to be You 121

64 The Truth of What I Do 122

65 To Share the Secrets of a Life 124

66 You Want a Reason to Cry?.. 125

67 They Don't Understand and They Don't Want To 128

68 Why Do I Want to Be a Girl?..131

69 I Am a Girl Now 134

70 A Boy I Never Told I Loved So He Could Stay My
Friend... 136

71 Everything Is Different... 138

72 Have a Good Cry 140

73 I Am Who I Am..142

74 I Walk Away... 144

75 Questions Answered 146

76 Girl in Love... 158

77 What Happens When You Finally Don't Care What
Others Think of You 160

78 Goodbye, Mom 161

79 Gender Euphoria 164

80 Quieting Down.. 166

81 Hi, Timmie.. 167

82	Love Learned Silently	169
83	You Can't Not Be	175
84	I Stand at Night	177
85	I Am a Girl	178
86	I Am on the Path	181
87	Finally Want a Man	183
88	The Trauma of It All	185
89	There Is No Such Thing as a Foolish Dream	189
90	Finish Becoming a Girl	191
91	I Will Never be Alone as Long as There is You	194
92	How Bad Do You Want to be a Girl?	196
93	Hi	199
94	Return	202
95	Homeless	204
96	The Psychology of Me	208
97	It's Hard to Write a Poem Right Now	211
98	Hi, Again	213
99	Looking Back	216
100	Looking Forward	221
101	I Don't Make Men Tingle	224
102	I Stand Alone	227
103	Sexuality	231
104	The Last Talk to Myself	234

The Reason for the Bangor Daily News Article ... 239
I Will No Longer Edit Me ... 257

Foreword

Talking to Myself: Poems from a Transgender Woman during Transition is a must read for anyone who is interested in the complex truth of the human condition and the nature of honesty.

The poems are raw, emotional, uninhibited, and beautifully honest. As a reader I found myself trying to fathom Sullivan's life from the beginning until now. It is an amazing journey. Sullivan doesn't dwell on her obvious intelligence or professional success—she was clearly very capable and highly successful at whatever she set her mind to. What she focuses on is her inner struggle and the eventual permission she gave herself to become the person she now is in both mind and body. This is no light matter, especially when many of the surgeries occurred when she was in her late sixties until now, at seventy-one.

I can only have respect for someone who has suffered so much at the hands of her family, colleagues, ex-wife, and former friends, and yet there is an abiding beauty on the path to her full realization of herself.

For those who are unsure of who they are the collection, by virtue of its honesty, has a didactic quality—and the lesson is clear, be who you are. Be true to what you know to be the authentic you. Surely this is a lesson for all of us who have experienced binary societal conditioning, and yet intuitively know that life is far more complex and nuanced than we ever believed possible.

From a literary perspective, the 'poems' do not always have the truck of formal poetry, but why should they? The collection is a series of experiences and moments that Sullivan has needed to pen and has also been courageous enough to share.

I read the collection as a cis-gendered male on my own journey of self-discovery. As such I found it a refreshing reminder that we are all on the journey to self to a greater or lesser degree, and at the same time, I realized that some journeys take a tremendous amount of strength and honesty to undertake. Such is Sullivan's journey. It is rich, complex, painful, and yet at the same time there is a beauty to it.

Perhaps she is now the girl she always knew she was—though she may not be. Life is not simple.

Whatever conclusion you come to, you will certainly be reminded that you, too, are on the journey, and you will be left questioning your own self-honesty, as well as commending Sullivan for hers. This is a must read.

Chris Marres

Preface

I spent my life wanting to be a girl. From the age of four, I was confronted by outside voices telling me, "You are not a girl." As I grew, I learned that this desire to be a girl had to be hidden and not talked about. The unspoken and hidden desire never abated. I was a girl; I was a girl in heart and mind, and I approached life with the emotional sensitivities of a girl.

I fell in love with boys; I did not fall in love with girls. During my male life, I told three different men that I was really a girl, and that I wanted to be their girlfriend. None of them ever talked to me again.

I retired from a professional career as a public health veterinarian, and I began the "freedom to grow old and die" period of life. My unhappiness from never being allowed to become a girl, nor having children, led to my becoming an alcoholic with near-death visits to the emergency room.

I informed my wife I was going to become a girl and that I was not asking permission—I was informing her. I am now divorced. I discovered that becoming a girl didn't cure my alcoholism. However, after several weeks in detox and several months in Alcoholism Recovery Camp, I am sober now. I am a sober girl.

So many decisions I made in life were greatly influenced by my actually being a girl in hiding. My relationships with my fellow men were odd to say the least. My relationships with women were equally odd in that I often looked to them for fashion sense and makeup tips, and that was something I did my whole life—long before I became a girl myself.

I am no longer an unhappy, suicidal, alcoholic, and unfulfilled man with few friends. I am now a happy, stable, sober, and beautiful girl. I wish that for everyone.

Initiating my transition was the most momentous decision of my life. The stress, the challenges, and the emotional difficulties led to many poems of sorrow, grief, and loneliness—and the discovery of happiness. These poems are presented in the chronological order of their being written, with few exceptions. The individual poems capture the moment that they were written, and are unique to that moment.

This book should be read by anyone and everyone. This is a rather self-serving thing for me, as the author to say, but this book contains the power of personal truths and honesty. Maybe through reading these poems, one will learn of the actual sincerity of individuals suffering from gender dysphoria and become more tolerant. Individuals who suffer from gender dysphoria, or are at some point in the process of transition, may find common threads of pain and hope. Comfort can be found within these poems as I share the blossoming of the girl I believe I always was.

I am Lukcia Patricia Sullivan, and I am not a poet; I am a woman who braved the elements of transition that confront anyone of similar pursuits. Maybe these poems are not poems, but rather short stories that lead into a moment of transition. Please don't read these poems in one sitting or even a few sittings. With few exceptions, these poems are in chronological order as written during my transition, so the beginning of the book is early in transition and the end of the book is at the completion of transition—at least physically.

Many poems have similar titles and similar threads of thought, but every poem is unique to a moment, unique to a specific element of stress or joy. Please take your time in reading each poem, try to feel that which I was experiencing, and revisit poems as they expose more of my truths and true nature.

These poems, and my psychologist, saved me from alcoholism and suicide. Alcoholism and suicide are very common in the transgender community.

Introduction

I sat on the edge of my bed and cried. I had started hormone replacement therapy and was now estrogen-based. My wife informed me that she would initiate divorce proceedings soon. Many lectures of "Why?" and "Stop!" and "Don't do this!" filled this initial period of time. I knew I couldn't turn back; I knew only suicide lay on the other side of that decision, so I cried for what I knew was coming—the pain and the loss of friends, but also the happiness I also knew was ahead of me.

As my tears rolled down my face, I had great emotions of such an internally challenging manner that I started to write what I was going through. This was initially just blurbs of thought, but soon, a poem appeared. I had written a truth of me. I had written of something so deep and hidden that I cried as this piece of me came out.

I revisited that poem several times over the next few days, and I cried at every reading. I knew that what I had done was to create a truth; a truth of me, my spirit, my heart, my soul, and my love. I knew that I needed to remember these truths as the challenges before me attempted to erase my courage.

I started writing a poem every time my emotions demanded that a truth be captured for future support. I had no intention of collecting the poems and publishing this book. I was just trying to stay alive. Try becoming a girl at age sixty-seven, watch your life melt away, know that courage can sometimes be weak, and know that you need to never forget your very personal truths. It's been hard—it's been really hard.

If I didn't revisit my truths, I may have revisited suicide. My truths of who I really am carried me through.

I don't think I am unique. I think many people with gender dysphoria experience the same difficulty. My poems literally saved my life. Not everyone writes their own personal truths. So, I am sharing mine. There is much of me in these poems: secrets never told, hopes until now out-of-reach, and maybe a lifeline to others to understand themselves or others going through transition.

I hope this book helps people as the poems have helped me.

Victor Stabin: The Turtle Series

I lay in bed recovering from my second vaginoplasty, a revision of the primary vaginoplasty one year eight months earlier. I was in The GAIA House, a B&B operated by Dr. Christine McGinn, my surgeon and sister in transition. Dr. McGinn transitioned many years ago when she was an Air Force Fight Surgeon. Dr. McGinn opened up a medical practice dedicated to the medical support of those in need of gender confirmational surgery. Her medical practice and The GAIA House are in New Hope, PA. The GAIA House is there only for her patients, and that is where I stayed during my many appointments leading up to, during, and after my transition.

The GAIA House is adorned with many of Victor Stabin's "The Turtle Series" prints. Every bedroom has one or two prints hanging, and the rest of the house has a several more.

At the time of my last surgery, I was nearing completion of this book. I was in my favorite room where a large print of the "The Secret Life of Turtles" hung. I realized that this print, along with the others, was critical to my mental health during the difficult times of transition.

Gender transition is both physically and emotionally difficult. I undertook this extremely challenging process of becoming a female at the age of 67. The Secret Life of Turtles spoke to me as I left behind that secret aspect of my life, to become Lukcia. The image is so joyful, so full of fantasy, and as Victor described it: a party we're not invited to. That was my life; living outside a party that I was not invited to, until now.

All of Victor Stabin's Turtle Series prints are beautifully done, complex, they invite one into the imagery in a meditative manner, and they are all soft in their language of acceptance and tolerance. The "Patron Saints of Perpetual Vision" is the cover of this book, and it helped me see my path to a future as a girl. The prints "Red Socks" and "Christy and Tom" also mean so much to me it is difficult to explain, but I found a quiet peace in the prints.

It is this author's hope that you enjoy the illustrations within this book. Hopefully you see and feel the joy, the hope, the dreamy state of somewhere special; a place where one can be their real self. Victor Stabin's prints are so playful and happy, while being without end in the provocation of contemplative thought.

Victor Stabin's art work can be seen at:

https://www.victorstabin.com/stabin-museum/
Lukcia Patricia Sullivan

Patron Saints of Perpetual Vision

I Lost My Mother

Some time ago my mother died.
She left me,
No longer by my side.
I knew I loved her;
I always said so!
Yet it was so different.
No longer there, no longer a soft voice
Saying she loved me too!
I lost my mother,
And I don't know quite when.
Was it when I left to freedom, or
Was it in college with all new friends?
Was it when I thought of her
Only now and then?
I lost my mother.
She left me before I left her.
She became the victim of life's
Negligence.
She died alone in a bed
Reserved for the already dead.
I wasn't there.
I was off on my career.
I stopped
To only start to realize
I lost my mother.
Time, time heals most wounds.
It took so long.
I found my mother.
She is in me.
She still shows me how to cook.
She still holds me on her side.
She still tells me to stand with pride.

I found my mother
Through a thousand memories
Woven throughout all of my life.
I am her daughter,
Lukcia Patricia Sullivan.
Thank you, Mom.

I Really Like Being a Girl

I really like being a girl
With silky, shaven skin,
Long hair with a little curl,
Polished fingers, and polished toes.

I really like being a girl.
Am I doing this right?
A girl doesn't happen overnight.
A girl to think, a girl to feel.

I really like being a girl.
Am I girl because I say so?
Will I never be a girl?
Will I ever know?

I really like being a girl.
Sixty-eight years out of sight
Now in full daylight.
My joy, my tears, are sincere. Is this girl real?

I really like being a girl.
I don't miss the male me.
I don't miss the *him* and *he*.
Away from him, I'm finally free.

I really like being a girl.
A pink skirt gracing shaven legs,
Sandals pretty, and toes pink.
A blouse, just enough. Think.

I really like being a girl.
Oh,
Did I mention
I really like being the girl
Lukcia Patricia Sullivan?

Courage

Oh! I sit looking out my window
at the challenges I am soon to face.

Yes! The same challenges
I have faced my whole life.

Hurray! I finally have courage
to face not just you but me too.

Oh! For so long facing you was off the table
because I couldn't face myself.

That's right! I was in denial to not only you
but also hiding from myself.

Now I step into my future with hopes
that went unfulfilled since their birth.

Alas! I no longer need to face you,
It is critical I learn to face myself.

Hallelujah! Contrary values no longer phase me.
I am so esoterically in my own place.

Crying! I look back with such sadness;
why not brave in the first place?

Finally! I have found the courage,
retired and old with so little left to lose.

Guess what! "So little" is still more than nothing, and
that "little" is critical to how I leave this place.

Guess what! I am Lukcia! I am Lukcia! I am Lukcia!
Oh, did I mention I am Lukcia?

I Never Got to Be a Girl Until Now

I never got to be cute and ever-so shy.
I never got to be someone's sweetheart,
Long before knowing why.
I never got to be a girl.

I never got to twitter with girlfriends.
I never got to discuss secrets that
Seemed to never end.
I never got to be a girl.

I never got to be soft, vulnerable.
I never got to be strong, sly,
Perfect a twinkling of the eye.
I never got to be a girl.

I never got to experience the stress
Of becoming a young lady,
A girl in transition.
I never got to be a girl.

I never got to be, to live, as a young lady.
I never got to say only "maybe."
The virtue of holding reserve.
I never got to be a girl.

I never got to tentatively and selectively date.
I never got to say, "You are late!"
To hold off at arm's length.
I never got to be a girl.

I never got to make the cardinal mistake
And give what was not ready to take,
To wail and wallow in fear.
I never got to be a girl.

I never got to break up with my first love.
Special naivete like a velvet glove.
To watch as a child dreams fade.
I never got to be a girl.

I never got to go to school,
Trying hard to be pretty and cool,
To attend to every fashion rule.
I never got to be a girl.

I never got the chance to squat to pee,
To know what to do with still wet nails.
Purses: OMG. What are the rules?
I never got to be a girl.

I never got married in white with
Everyone telling me I am beautiful tonight.
Raise the veil and kiss a man while others hail.
I never got to be a girl.

I never got to be a mother to anyone.
Sadly, I never got to be a parent with
Grandchildren in my front yard.
I never got to be a girl.

I never got to face the challenge,
To be who I am not, to live as I want.
Transgender. Not hard. Alone in my own backyard.
I never got to be a girl.

I did get to be sad about what I couldn't be.
I did get to wish I had to squat to pee.
I did get to keep a secret, hidden me.
I never got to be a girl.

I did finally get the chance.
Come out, come out, come out, and dance.
Allowed to be only recently
A girl—no, a woman now.

A woman now, a female.
What do "fe" and "male" have to do with me?
"Wo" and "man" also pisses off me.
I am a girl.

I am a girl—there's no other word.
Don't dare "wo" or "fe" me.
I am not of your rib, you prick.
I finally got to be a girl.

Decisions

I am walking the path to you.
The you the future me wants to be.

Silly in my lack of fear.
Untested confidence in the worth of you.

Not a difficult path for me.
All who love me, or care, find me obscure.

When I am alone
Wallowing in hope unknown,

So crisp and clear is my goal:
For you know there is no *there*.

Never a woman be
Praying to be a facsimile.

They laugh; I do too.
I pray they don't laugh at you.

Change is slow.
A lifetime devoted here.

Technology catalyzed.
Now a lifetime and one year.

Alone, I grow to be you.
Other's embrace fraught with fear.

Soon: medical marvels.
I enter the gauntlet and emerge as you.

I love you, Lukcia.
I hope you love you too.

Bernard vs. Lukcia
What Is a Brand-New Girl to Do?

Bernard, Bernard, Bernard.
Sixty-eight years walking this earth.
Sixty-eight years had to be a
Gentleman, a man.

Bernard, frail and blind.
Couldn't see ball, hit with bat.
Aware of environment within one foot—be
Outside that.
Blurred history.

Bernard and mother really close.
Security, understanding, a safe host.
Safety slowly slides away;
Other forces have sway.

Bernard stays, a baby be.
Departure must occur to otherwise be.
Environment of a youthful boy.
Entered frail, a boy toy.

Bernard's abuse and joy.
How to know the difference?
Learning curve soft and hidden and slow.
Still don't know.

Bernard the individual.
Confronting strife and life.
Challenge the now; challenge stability.
Life to copacetic be.

Lost: man or reality.
First: reality, the man, or me?
At this point I had no idea how to survive.

A man to you; a girl to me.

Lukcia, Lukcia, Lukcia.
Sixty-eight years walking this earth.
Sixty-eight years hidden.
Girl, a woman be.

No longer let you rule.
No longer adopt the values of a fool.
To be me, to be me, with
No idea who I am.

Walk away.
So much Bernard—
Never him, never good.
Understood?

Happy, happy, happy.
Oh, it sounds too happy to be.
Many moments of tranquility.
Dream realized.

Moving from and to
A dream, reality: I was there.
No longer there at last.
Lukcia born with a storied past.

So much of him has
Fallen away, erased in minds.
Friends to only Bernard.
Lukcia alone: free.

Oh! To dress
Talk, walk, be a girl.
Challenge and delight.
Finally, me.

Wear a bra.
Young breasts pout.

Wear a skirt.
Shaved legs all the way out.

Meet a boy—
A man, actually.
Know that I could love,
Love as me.

Wife and life.
Things don't last.
Start a new life. Start a new life.
Start a new life as a wife.

Now up to where I am.
Now up to, "Can you really be?"
Don't know but won't survive
Returning to *you know who*.

I Always Wanted to Be a Girl

I always wanted to be a girl.
I never wanted to be a boy.
I didn't hate being a boy.
I didn't know to
Hate something then.
I didn't want to go there.
I didn't want to be
With him and him and he.
I didn't want to live
Within the expectations of
All the hims and all the hes.
I was already a girl so early.
Not yet a *her* or *he*.
Over the years the *he* was imposed.
Her was not disposed.
Silenced, she stepped back.
She, the me in she,
Never left me.
This all happened before I was ten.
Since then, since then,
I am old but not worn out.
Now I am going to let *her* out.
I have so little time left.
No one knows how much.
The rest of my life I will be
She, her, girl: my destiny.
Everyone, literally everyone
Thinks I am crazy.
A woman alone, better than an
Unhappy man.
I can't explain the truth of
How I feel.
A short skirt makes me happy.
Shaved legs to feel.
To the love of polished nails,
Love beyond compare.

I put on my wig;
Hair down to there.
Young breasts still growing.
I love them there.
Life in a small town
Over twenty years.
Everyone knows
I have gone queer.
No one says a word.
No one says what I am doing is
Bad.
In silence, I lost every
Old friend I had.
Ready, so ready
To walk alone.
Alone: this will not stop me.
Of course, prefer company.
Never again will I be
Someone to fit in with.
You, and he, and he, and he
I walk away from all the hims, all the hes,
To do what I have begun.
Intensity—
Intensity to be.
Intensity to unsilence me as "She."
Change scares so many off.
I dream of her, the future me.
She is stable.
She is happy.
I think I will be OK.
I want to be a woman, but I also
Want to be OK.
What strange letters to describe.
I am good as me.
This poem will never end.
The path is still before me.
I speak of life.
I am Lukcia!

No Poem Tonight

Tonight, I am not going to write you a poem;

I am going to sit quietly, all alone.

More than I was; less than I want to be.

Stuck between old friends and friends I am yet to meet.

The old friends will become history.

How does one explain me?

This stage of transition carries so much pain

As I step away from yesterday, and wish …

To be here and there,

To be now and so long ago,

To be Lukcia, and wish Lukcia is who you were.

No.

I am not a revisionist; I can't rewrite the past.

Lukcia is the product of sixty years of pain.

If she was then, she would not be the same.

I sit here now, dinners done.

I explained myself yet again.

Alone ... yes, alone,

With quiet thoughts.

I am finally with Lukcia.

I will be OK.

Fish Ferris Wheel

The Private Nature of What I Do

This is a path to walk alone …

This is a path to walk …

This is a path.

Alone … not to atone.

Shed support of selfish needs.

Shed support of

Private greeds.

Alone … not to atone.

Walk forward into unknown.

Walk forward into

Alone.

Alone … not to atone.

I can handle alone.
Here, it's a tool;

Centers me.

Alone … not to atone.

No one injured by my next step.

No one injured yet.

Not injured—an impossibility.

Alone ... not to atone.

I don't want you there.

You are not to know

My path.

The path that belongs only to me.

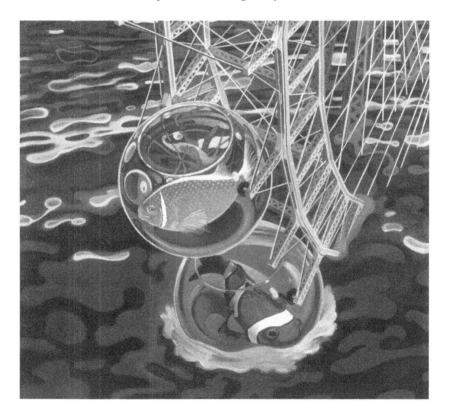

A Girl Maybe

To be a girl,
You have to be really here.
You can't become a girl
And harbor fear.

I have always been a girl;
I have never been a girl.
Cis women don't understand.
No sense, non-sense—I can see it too.

I leave male misogyny
To become more exposed
As Lukcia,
Subject to a second level of cruelty.

It's OK;
I will do my best.
Every time I meet a man—
Ah!—pass the test.

Another Transgender Woman

I hope you are experiencing something special.

You are now you.

For a year now,

I float in a sea

Of the future: Lukcia.

Oh!

I am sure you did too.

Slowly ... softly,

Flow into you.

Rest.

Then rest.

There will be enough time to

Push the quest.

I love you ...

Ahhh.

I am where you were,

But for me, it was thirty years ago.

Think soft thoughts now;

Don't think about the courage

That got you here.

Think.

Think

About the pillow talk

You might have now.

Talking to Lukcia

I get closer and closer
To where you are.

How will you feel when that morning
You step into the car?

Travel ... too soon ... too late?

Step into a paid-for fate?

Walk through glass doors,
Down corridors; corridors

Lay back silent.

Are you OK?

Of course, it is "yes."
There is no other way.

A very polite person
Talks to you.

Count back from ninety-nine.

Ninety-nine ... ninety-eight ... ninety-seven ... ninety ... six ...

Totally Under Control

I know you and I are just good friends.
I am using you to help me train me.
What better classroom than an understanding friend?
I am going to be a girl ... and when you see ...
The future me ...
You will convey ...
"On me, she practiced that."
Don't worry, friend.
Beyond a point,
You won't find me.
I barely am here.
For now,
Here is where I need to be.
Let me be pretty.
Then, let me get ready to bike.
Let me kit up,
Ride alongside you.
Let me be Lukcia,
And still alongside you,
Pop a beer.

The story ends here.
I am good with "here."

To My Psychologist

Tonight, I still need to thank you.
OK ... I always will.
Tonight, you were supportive in a different way,
Weaning me off you
Like a calf calling for its mother.
I am that calf.
I am calling out.
I am aware I have to grow up now.
I am not a calf, but I am also not a cow.
I am going to need you
Way past our last visit.
You are now in me.
Your soft acceptance—
That acceptance will carry me
As I apply it to my future.
Finally ... Finally,
A person that goes beyond understands.
My heart erupts
When someone accepts me.
I have so many faults,
Even I could reject me.
It's your job to be with me,
But I believe you see the real me.
This poem, it wanders.
It goes where it might.
I believe in you,
Because you believe in me.

Alcoholism Recovery Camp

I can't go back.
The men are too mean; the women too abused.
My heart goes too them.
But still ...
I need to be there.
I need to be there ... there ... still.
I have to be here.
Here—to fight my private war.
I can't be there.
I so wish I was.
So private am I now.
I can't be there.
The shame is too great.
I don't know how to step away from me ...
A space in time, so I can cry ...

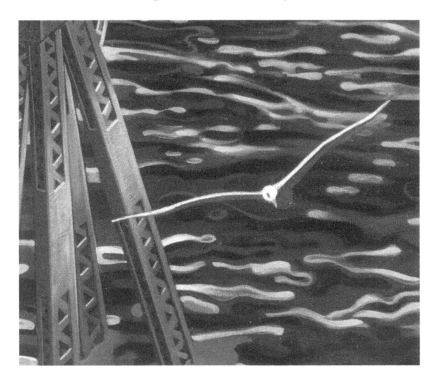

Hair

Tonight, another night.
Can't take off my hair.
While not my hair,
It's on my head.
Right now,
It needs to stay there.
Long and blond,
Pretty as can be.
Framed face,
So happy.
It's time; it's time
To go to bed.
I sit on the edge;
View my image in black glass instead.
I used to be
Bald—my earlier reality.
Blond hair flows now,
Down to my breasts.
I am Lukcia now.
Lukcia has blond hair.
If taken off,
Am I no longer there?
I feel how fragile
My new girl be.
This beautiful spell
Broken too easily.
I know when I sleep,
I need to undress.
Peeling Lukcia away:
Sometimes too big a test.
Those nights, I sleep
In my skirt ... bra and panties.
Sleep clothed like this.
He doesn't creep into my dreams.
Lukcia is more fragile
Than she seems.

In the morning,
Hair a mess,
Panties in a knot—
Now I know what that means—
Lukcia awakes and enters
Another day.
Lukcia, Lukcia; I know
You're here to stay.
Damn, I wish I had
hair!

A Poem for Ranay

The path to "girl" is long … You always knew you
belonged … So, it didn't make difference how long.

Every day I step forward and say, "I am one
step closer to Lukcia or Ranay."

There have been too many steps … too many days … too many preps.

I never see those too many be; I only see today, and someday girl be.

To be sad about a past you gave up is stupid; you never gave up.

Be twenty-nine or ninety-two: not allowed to prioritize the actual you.

I am not becoming a girl, and neither are you; I am already, and so are you.

Many tolerated my love from a secret place: the place wishing a girl be.

So many men I treated fine; only learned "Don't cross this line."

Only cis women cross the line; only cis women allowed beyond "fine."

Don't know what "cis woman" means, but they know it isn't me.

The Challenge of Taking So Long

I wish it didn't take so long.
It took too long to suppress me as a little girl.
It took too long for me to see
I had to hide her deep inside me.
I wish it didn't take so long
To meet a childhood friend, and to be so close.
It took too long for me to realize
Boyhood friends are not like me.
I wish it didn't take so long
To meet a girl and think, *There is compatibility.*
For so long, I said yes to a night with a girlfriend
While wishing I could wear her dress.
I wish it didn't take so long
To so carefully build a social community,
To explain myself, and dissolve that community.
I wish it didn't take so long
To find a safe place in the military.
It didn't take long for so many of them to see
A girl to harass, and rape with glee.
I wish it didn't take so long
To learn to better hide the real me.
It took too long for me to crush, to collapse
The beautiful person living inside me.
I wish it didn't take so long
To marry someone as selfish as me.
I was never a good husband-to-be;
Married just to have a girl's dream of family.
I wish it didn't take so long
To explain to my wife who I really was.
Too long: opportunities lost—
For her as much as me.
I wish it didn't take so long
To learn to teach others of the hidden me.
It took so long to lose friends, because I didn't know how
To explain me.
I wish it didn't take so long

To find the courage to seek professional help.
To finally cry, and cry, and cry … hard,
Fully exposing my hidden self.
I wish it didn't take so long
To find the professionals I needed to support me.
So long ago, there was no one there.
When I finally asked, many were there for me.
I wish it didn't take so long
To determine that I am sincere.
So long, I held quiet this lifelong fantasy,
Believed me the first day required a year.
I wish it didn't take so long
To fully transition, to schedule the new me.
Too long to sit alone, wanting to be.
Alone again, to question a lifelong dream.
I wish it didn't take so long
To train "untrue he" … and hidden "she."
Too long to train the new freedom of "she."
Transition is bootcamp for a transgender girl.
I wish it didn't take so long.
I really wish it didn't take so long.
Long is hard, long is tough.
Lukcia is one tough girl.

Tough Night

Too many people let me know where I stand.
I am easily as nice as them, but they are already part of the band.
I very much know I have some tough times ahead.
I am more worth knowing now, but conversation's
slightly better than with a cow.
Oh ... it's not sour grapes.
I have to also reject ...
Reject sour grapes.
I have to wait for a special space,
A special man ... special place.
Maybe a woman, maybe only me.
I will take me as Lukcia, without hesitation.
Nothing for me will work without me,
And as my only close friend, I will be OK.
Sometimes I am the only one I like anyway.
I spent my life in rooms alone.
Most I knew walked past or straight through.
I now sit in those same rooms.
The same rooms, alone.
They a friend to you; zombie to me.
I needed, yet no one there.
I have learned: only me.
Wife almost exactly the same.
Now she is with distain.
I, the man others feign not to see.
In front of you, still, transparency.
Never again fake—just don't see me.
I am stronger than most.
I stand right in front of the firing squad's post.
I continue to generous be, while I curse your feigned legitimacy.
I am in a zoo of one cage, one stage ... one of my construct.
Oddly enough, so are most of you.

Feeling Like a Girl

So often, I feel so much like a girl.
Can't explain it.
I like it so much.
Just thought I would share that with you.
When I go into my "girl," really comfortable there,
I am so "so there."
You know, being a girl isn't about being a girl to someone else;
It's about being a girl to yourself.
It is so strange to decide I know ... what it means to be a girl,
Because I will actually never know.
I am at peace with the girl I found. She ... she ... me! Yes, I am her.
I want world peace; I want tranquility.
I want what all young women long to be.
I am on the other side of that naivete.
I have circled back; Yes ... that is the right thing to say.
I want to Miss America be to at least one man, a man who crowns me.
So foolish, so foolish I seem to be.
Why fifteen more years of unhappy?
Just today alone, my nails polished red; in my sleep,
I will dream of them instead.
Oh, believe me ... I know it will get rough.
Look to my smile.

Hatchlings

I Want to Be a Girl

What is it—Wanting to be a girl?
A "girl"; it never starts at "woman."
No, it starts at "girl."
No, not later.
Only, maybe before.
What is a truth?
Something you know from your first breath
Or what you're told during all the rest?
I am a girl ... I have always been ...
The part that loves me is the "her" within.

Coming True

Hot damn!
Breaking through.
Girl: coming true.
Months to go.
So close, so close!
Clean up act,
Walk straight,
Take seriously.
Not too late!
Everything was:
Out of reach.
Years: don't try.
Hide.
What can I say ...?
Hide.
Can I be—
Can I be more?
Than he?
Now ...
In months,
I will be a she.
The challenge, now,
Is to believe in
Me.
Once,
Back in '73,
I dreamed of being
A Fa'afafine.
Once, one
Noticed
I noticed her.
She came ...
Evening with me.
No,
Nothing occurred.
Two girls,

Sitting together
On a
Accepting log.
I saw her.
She saw me.
One night:
Bliss.
I almost
Was me.
That was fifty years
Ago.
Fifty years ...
One evening,
I saw me.
Now,
I step
Into the fire,
Fulfill
Primal desire.
I can't look back;
I can't allow
Me to see
How comfortable
Hiding came to be.
Don't do it!
Don't do what you want.
Look down,
Close your eyes,
Move into your
Preapproved destiny.
No.
A second time.
No.
So ...
You are not
What you want to be.
Maybe a loser
With history.
Maybe successful.
Nothing off shelf.

How often
Are you asked
What you actually
Want to be?
How often
Have you asked yourself
What
I
Want to be?
Soon,
I become a girl—
A miracle
Of surgery.
I have fears;
Few regrets.
I spent my whole life
He
When
Her
Was me.
I can't
Be afraid now
To live.
A hidden
She
Took
Much
Courage,
Keeping
Her alive.
Silently,
I hope
I survive
Becoming her
In
Five months.
Talk
To me.
I am Lukcia Patricia Sullivan.

End of Your Life

Look!
See!
The end of your life.
Knowing it is there
Too often
Doesn't change a thing.
At nineteen years of age,
I almost died
In a typhoon's rage.
At twenty,
I laid in wilderness,
Fighting off an OD.
At twenty-one,
The wheels came off.
Low, low,
How low can one go?
At twenty-two,
I was lost.
Lost to more than you,
I was lost to me.
At twenty-three,
I had a baby girl—
A girl I would never see.
At twenty-four,
junior college.
Turn this ship around!
From twenty-four to thirty-five:
Study hard,
Barely survive.
At thirty-six,
Married and in the army.
I spent my earlier life
Alone.
Married now,
But no one's home.
From then

To not too long ago,
I did what
I was told to do.
I did what justified
You
Knowing me—
In a box
Or in a lane,
Stay.
I stay somewhere
I never wanted to be.
At sixty-eight,
I clearly see
The end of life
Approaching me.
So many times, I survived
Death's grasp.
Now,
Too much inevitability.
Now,
This is the time
To make a change,
To stop
Being whom they want
You to be.
I am on a path,
Hoping to find
The true me.
Not your me;
I did that for years,
Quite successfully.
This path, in conflict
With most everything.
The path screams
Questions at me:
Who are you?
Who do you want to be?
The end of life is a power.
See it ... Learn.
There is no second turn.

I hope
The end of your life
Brings to you
As much power as
It brought to me.
It is so easy to be weak
When
Every day you must be strong,
To stay
On a path,
A path that's yours alone.
Apparently, the operative word is
Alone.

Thank You for Yesterday

I didn't email you
To thank you for today.
Now it is tomorrow.
A late thank you:
Too bad; It's all your fault.
Yesterday was special.
Tears were not
Sad.
Everything talked about
To get here—
The work
We had to do,
How
After so many hours,
Finally, finally glad.
Every tear a gift,
A gift from me to me.
You helped
Me give
The gift I couldn't see.
A girl soon.
Healthy.
You beside,
I found
A glimpse of me.
Know ... know
A ways to go.
Prayer is a way
To not take responsibility.
Guess what?
I don't pray.
Dead tomorrow ...?
That's OK.
I wouldn't have it
Any other way.
I owe nobody

Anything.
The point is,
If I don't complete
This path,
Does it matter
If I am here?

Trademark

Love

I am a girl, but I wasn't a girl before.
One of the reasons to become a girl was to learn what love means again.
I used to think I knew, but years challenged my ability to.
I learned love so long ago—
Not the word love, but so much more.
The word love is so cheap; if you can't see past the word, you don't know.
I think the first person to teach me love was my mom.
I was too young to know the word.
She gave me the gift of sensitivity,
To feel the tingle of love in an open way.
The first time I felt love and felt I knew
The gift of love—from a cat.
Panther Puss, a jet-black cat, a stray with a broken leg,
Injured, in the barn, I cared for him every day.
I learned what I felt for that cat was love.
That cat taught me how I felt about my mom.
I didn't feel love again for many years.
Love is so much more than a word.
I met a young man; his name was Charles.
We were both young; it was 1973.
In my heart, I was his girl, but that possibility was fifty years away.
After almost two years of just him and me,
I told him how I felt.
He turned and walked away; together, that was the last day.
Something similar happened a few more times.
Love is so difficult to see, so difficult to feel, even more difficult to share.
I became a veterinarian, because a cat taught me how to know love.
My mom taught me how to love, long before I knew the word.
I need to go back to that time to find me.
Loving before knowing what love was,
Flowing into the joy of something so felt as true,
Why do I care about love so much?
Let me tell you about something that cat
taught me, and every animal since:
Love is the only universal currency.
Love will carry you past your death.

Love is the fiber of gold that links everyone
willing to see, maybe only feel.
Take the lesson the cat gave me,
Close your eyes in a relaxed manner;
After you are quietly behind your lids,
Settle yourself and learn to purr.
As you purr, don't do anything.
Wait ... Wait ... let your heart reach out.
Don't think for a minute I am teaching you how to love.
I am only trying to teach you how to see.
Love was there the whole time, just waiting for you.
Once you see the golden fibers that link everyone and everything,
Everyone before and past is linked to you.
Don't try to see too much; if you see all the fibers, it blinds you to reality.
No, please start small ... Start with love ... Look for true,
Close your eyes and purr.
The golden fibers of love will soon be seen.

How Do I Change My Mind?

Transgender surgery:
Five weeks away; the first of a few.
I am so far out; all my friends know what I am about to do.
Some look at me sadly and say, "You know, you don't need to."
Others, "Are you going to go ... are you going to go through ...?"
Only a few say, "You go, girl!" and "I am so happy for you."
Of course, being confronted almost daily, even by a friend,
Causes me to rethink this irreversible plan.
So, I say "so" a lot, even when I am talking to myself.
So, because this decision is only for me, only I need care.
So, how do I change my mind?
How do I undo a year of discovering the me that's true?
I have to learn how to be happy while not happy
anymore; I was so unhappy before.
I most likely will have to decide I can no longer wear a dress.
Concerned friends suggest I do something in between:
Play girl at home; forget the rest.
When I go out, I really like to go "girl."
Lipstick, mascara, a little pink blush, my
diamond earrings, and so much more.
I guess I would have to give this up; it's on the "girl" side of in between.
Oh, let's not forget: I threw out three hundred
pounds of the clothes guys get.
Most of my new clothes are for going out—stepping out, strutting proud.
I have a lot invested now in being pretty.
So (there it is again), if I change my mind, do all
of my old friends come back in time?
I don't think so. I broke a rule one is not to break.
To them, personal discovery is fake.
My wife can never see me as "he" again, because
she knows I am truly a "she."
So, how do I change my mind?
Oddly enough, I still can; everything above is
only this last year of being "her."
Everything I have done I can't undo; as a veteran
of four wars, I am not afraid of any of you.

This last year has been me breaking through.
I wasn't in a closet; I was in Al Gore's lockbox, the only place I felt safe.
As hard as it will be to even slightly return to the earlier me,
It isn't hard, because of this last year.
So, how do I change my mind?
I would have to revisit the little girl that didn't know she wasn't one.
I would have to undo memories of dressing in my sister's clothes.
How do you undo kissing your first boy at the age of seven?
Every true love was another man, but me as
a girl they couldn't understand.
A lifetime of finding happiness with a few
days, or a week of wearing a dress?
Not really fitting in with other men; also, not fitting in with women.
So, life was no piece of cake—not being a man, but a man I must fake.
If I look back on him, there is no way I will change my mind.
Something special has happened to me.
I am looking at the world through the eyes
of the girl I always wanted to be.
I can sit now properly, as a good girl is meant to;
something I've waited so long to do.
I look out and see things as "pretty," I appreciate small things happily,
I even serve food as a girl; there is a difference
between Chef Him and Chef Her.
Fifty years since "he" first shaved "her" legs, legs
that will never again belong to him.
I don't just wear a skirt; I see a beautiful girl with
a skirt four inches above her knees,
And guess what ... I find her pretty.
I am so visually happy, because of how I see me but also how I see you.
The question of how do I change my mind is absurd.
I never changed my mind, since the first day I
knew I was a girl; that was in 1952.
Even if I am alone, I will be alone with the only true me.

Girl

Girl.
Girl: A simple word ... that doesn't have that four-letter word.

Girl,
Rise up and take back history.
Defined by the past is history,
Written by the four-letter word.

Girl.
I, myself, can't go back to be that four-letter word.
So, now the words that somewhat define me
Are without the "Wo" and "Fe" prefix; yes, I am free.

Girl,
What have you been through
That I wish I had been through too?
Do you have any idea how much I love you because you survived?

Girl.
Today's girls are so much more tough,
But it took yesterday's girls to toughen you up.
Do you know who they are; on whose shoulders you stand?

Girl.
Germaine Greer once came to me.
She was at the front of "Why do we let them be in charge?"
Men are small ... They all think they're large.

Girl,
That was a double entendre.
The "he" can no longer keep his fantasy
That he is better than me.

Girl,
I know I am asking to be who you are.
Fully ... Fully Understand,
I so already know I can never be.

Girl,
I am taking a stand for Transgender girls,
Because that is who I am.
All of us need to stand breast to breast.

Girl.
I will never truly be a girl, but get ready.
I will never say I am not.
Between me and "He" there was a gulf; between
you and me there is silken cloth.

Girl,
So, what am I asking of you here:
Give up the "Fe," give up the "Wo."
That is their shit here.

Girl!
Hey, Girl ... What be happening here?
Sister, you down with me, no longer defined by "Wo" and "Fe"?
Please see where I am going here.

Girl,
Girls matter.
Transgender Girls Matter.
Don't you want to matter too?

GIRL

Lipstick

I wore lipstick all day, a soft, slightly brownish pink.
My sister taught me how, along with how to use a little blush.
Everywhere today, my lips distinct; I was so happy to feel them that way.
I have been a girl for over a year, but lipstick has eluded me.
So does blush, so does shadow, so does eyeliner being kept narrow.
I love lipstick—I can feel it on me; it's there, my lips, dressed to see.
I am preparing my lips for the eventual kiss. I
want them ready to capture bliss.
A young girl's lips; that is what they are.
Does a girl feel a kiss differently?
Lipstick:
A silent promise of a kiss.

КYEOTB

I Don't Want to be Tough Anymore

I don't want to be tough anymore, even though I know I can.
I don't want to be tough anymore; it takes so much from me.
Being tough is tough; tough for every moment of who you are.
Tough defines me more than anything else.
I gave so much to be tough; I never again want it to be a part of me.
I was not perceived as tough, but as a subordinate to ...
Believe me, that was tough.
I never believed in me until some twenty years ago.
Another poem, another day; this poem is about being tough.
Tough is two paths, maybe three.
Maybe as Hawking says, "Infinity."
Tough is hide-and-seek where you can never be found.
Tough is of loves you can never say.
Tough is things, pretty and sweet, you don't
know—can't let anyone else know too.
Tough is never knowing when tough can go away.
I already know
Tough can never go away.
How does one undo what happened to me?
I am retired; four-war military, I have seen true misery.
Part of my PTSD is
I can never say I have PTSD.
It's not me; it's you all around me: no idea ... no idea.
I have had to separate myself from the "you."
I have had to form my own value structure too.
I care for what I care about; I can't care for something because you do.
How can I do that when you have no idea how much I love things
You think are unreal?
Every day, I walk out into a space that is a social-challenge place.
The poem returns to being tough.
What happens when you want to love people, but they don't know enough?
They don't know why sometimes you cry.
As a man, you cry way too much.
They don't know what I have seen, and seeing ...
Oh, God ... I wish I could only have seen.

How does one watch so many lose every dream?
Surrounded by misery, it was relatively easy to be tough.
Ignore everything past the eyes.
Shut down love ... Shut down sound.
Now, I am in the land of everything you want.
I can no longer be tough.

I Am Only Her, I Am Only She, I Am Only a Version of "He"

Oh, God, I cry too much.

I don't want to be a "her."

Never a "she."

Why is "he" in every word to describe me?

No.

I can't do it anymore.

I sit across from my ex-wife.

I can't do it anymore.

She is who I love.

She is who I want to be.

Tough as nails,

A statement she doesn't understand.

I am lost to her; she is lost to me.

How do you marry a girl who is who you want to be?

Maybe because you had no other choice.

How do you tell her you are leaving now because
you need to be as strong as her?

How do you say you loved her every day?

Every element of her is now a part of me.

I will never not want for her;

She can't tolerate the new me.

I prayed, I hoped, I tried so hard to be

Acceptable.

I am not.

I am not

To my wife.

What did I have to give to have given enough?

What love is a love that can never die?

What life is a life that passes in the blink of an eye?

I don't know.

I really wish I did.

I am so happy to be a girl, finally,

A girl no one else wants me to be.

It took time for me to write these words.

Nothing's new.

I step into me every day.
Thirty years ago ... no, forty years ago ... also no ... fifty years ago:

I was eighteen,

Stepping into life unseen.

That young man I can no longer be.

Courage is not gender-bound.

I am Lukcia.

Get out of the way!

I Am So Glad I Am Finally a Girl
or Looking Through the Eyes of He

I feel like I am finally there!
I am a girl, finally.
For so long, I had to work at it
To be a girl that was yet to be.
I could see that girl, the girl that was me,
Like a distant mirage, false water on the highway.
Into focus that girl had to come,
Closer and closer ... Until
The girl and me merge as one.
I think I merged now,
And as I type this I cry.
It's been such a hard journey.
You know,
I finally think I have PTSD,
Not from what happened to me,
But what I had to see,
Looking through his eyes.
The real world, no disguise,
I find myself sitting in a room with men.
Strange looks; one gets up and moves away.
I can't not see what he saw.
They cannot see me.
Am I becoming a girl to erase the he?
Yes, most definitely.
Am I becoming a girl to be a she?
That is where the question is wrong.
I am not becoming a girl to be a she;
I am becoming a girl to be me.
Through his eyes, I still see
Yard work, tractor repair, garden redress, and all the rest.
I can never not be good at what he did best.
He is gone; the girl will have to pass the test.
As a girl, when you work hard ... how do you dress?
I wish I could vacate him from me.

I am a girl one year; sixty-eight years was he.
I can never not look out through his eyes.
Even when I look at a mirror and a pretty girl see,
I am looking at me, and he is looking at me.
Do you know how hard it's been?
Do you have any idea what I have been through?
I see old friends with his eyes.
I walk up to them in disguise.
I challenge them for a minute or two
To accept me as a girl.
Please.
None of you know where I have been.
None of you know what I have been through.
I have been so many places I never want to return to.
I never want to return to him.
I am finally a girl.
Now, I need to learn to see
Life as a girl, as a girl would see.
I am finally a girl.
That girl you see?
That girl is me.

I Think I Am Going to Be a Bitch

Any idea what I do?
Any idea what I am going through?
What happens
When ...?
Live the secret you.
"Oh, great," you say.
Suppressed the easier way.
Marriage sucked.
Normal; yours does too.
I am not unique ...
Not just transgender speak.
Relationships
Continue,
Easier than "dis."
Freedoms: another word.
Freedom: absurd.
Nothing to lose.
Lose ... lost it yesterday.
Nothing ain't nothing
If you lose you.
Today, I celebrate
The freedom to be
Me.
Cautiously
Approved
Surgeries:
Few years ago;
Not there.
Modern society
Challenges
Those who dare.
Girl,
Do I dare?
Girl,
Yes.
Not ...

Option.
Not …
Not going where
I belong.
Before couldn't—
Now …
Can.
Gosh …
Scary.
I can't wait to be a girl.
Yes, it's scary, but I am so ready.
Give me a new face, give me larger breasts,
Give me a vagina that will pass the "are you a man" test.
Damn.
I think I am going to be a bitch.

Transgender Pain

You need to spend more time with me

To see how much pain I am in.

I don't step across a line between your property and mine.

I become someone I don't know.

I believe most of her will be the base of me—

Uncharted territory.

I no longer am in charge of him, of her, of any of my tomorrows.

I believe in my most basic me.

My most basic me is a girl.

Good bye, Lia.

I am no longer there for you.

I am no longer there for me.

I am in the turbulent river of my destiny.

Step up,

Step up.

Take charge of this article.

I no longer can even think.

He was here, but he is gone.

She is here, but how strong.

I have to remember.

Remember,

Remember,

I was never not a girl.

Red Socks

If You're Not Dead

Not everything is the product of "cry."

I was told today I passed all my pre-surgery tests.

"Are you nervous?" they say ... *No, I spent my life waiting for this day.*

"Are you worried how it will turn out?" they say ...

They don't understand ... these surgeries are saving me.

I was "he", and he was going nowhere fast.

That's what's cool about finally studying myself:

So many mistakes because I was someone else.

On the table, I could be dead; it would be better than what was ahead.

So many young men end their life because they couldn't be a girl.

Many that can, but are not accepted, end their life too.

Most no one wants to discuss; this is not something up to us.

Universally, all the "a girl I want to be" children know before they're four.

That is an age when truth is not yet scary.
I enter a significant medical test; if I don't survive, don't feel sorry for me.

I walked a life where I could always see

Death walking slightly to the left of me.

Wow, that was fun.

Talk about death to everyone.

Don't get me wrong … Death is a source of "happy."

If you're not dead, you still can be something else instead:

Lukcia.

Facial en Femme

One month to go to *facial en femme* surgery.
When I was young, fifty-plus years ago,
I was *en femme* almost naturally.
Now I am a girl, but him I still see.
I need to separate him from my new me.
I don't want to make people look past the "he"
In order to see the girl.
I don't want to do it too.
I need to see a unique "her" more easily.
Facial feminization surgery.
In a skirt, I am too often still called "sir."
He or her still a blur,
I want to be a girl someday and not have to explain "him" away.
I can go into the lady's room and not be called out.
Erase the "him", so she presides.
What's left of him is deep inside.
If any significant "him" remains,
He could rear his head and overcome "she."
I really need to not remember how to be "he."
I don't want to be him anymore.
Sixty-five years a "she" in the body of a man.
Do you have any idea how tough "she" had to be?
He did what was necessary;
I don't want to do that anymore.
Please, whatever God there is, please don't make me.
If there is trouble now, I want to run away.
Can a man protect me for at least one day?
I want to be the weaker sex,
A statement that dates me.
I don't want anyone to see me as a man.
I can see them see the earlier me.
From then on, I am a girl-facsimile.
How can I truly be me
If they, and sadly me too, think I am *acting* as a "she"?
I don't want to *act* like a girl; I want to *be* a girl.
Too much of this is in the mind.

My mind is sharp; my mind is not kind.
A lot of facial surgery, not to convince you.
First, I have to convince me.
This poem has helped me understand:
When I am done, I need to move away.
I don't think I am brave enough to stay.
No matter what face they see, I will know they still see "he."
Some with sad eyes, some with glee, some laughing … laughing
At me.
I wish everyone really knew me.
They don't understand to do "girl"
Took more courage than going to war.
If I stay, it will be hard to convince all the "thems"
I want to stay.
The only person I need to convince?
Me.

To Be in Love

I ask so many questions of myself,
To find my way, to see my path.
Decisions that never go away,
Each step taken can never be undone.
I am so past undo; can't undo done.
So, why do I do what I do?
I ask myself, as you ask me too.
I had a life, I had a wife, I had a place in polite society.
Now, I only have a life, but one that doesn't belong where I was.
I can tell you why I have done what I have done:
Only as a girl can I truly love someone.
Even when very young, I only wanted to feel as a girl—embraced,
Augmented lips to finally be kissed for real,
To coo into a lover's ear,
To feel another grope in lustful hope,
To be able to acquiesce without fear.
These are the things that brought me here.
Everything I have done, everything I do,
With only one goal in mind,
As a girl,
To be in love.

Arielle Eve

What I Can't Do

So long ago, I was so alone, hiding in the basement;
No one else home.
Larry would come to me and teach me how to be
The girl he wished I was.
I always wanted to be a girl, just not the one he saw in me.
We moved, and he was gone.
A year later, I was ten and became an altar boy.
Every day at five, I would bike to Sacred Heart
And pray.
I was so internalized, Larry taught me how to hide
In plain sight.
I became a person only to me; no one else could see.
They never looked, so it was easy.
So early, so very early in being me,
I answered to no one else, only me.
Walking a path where no one tells you where to step—
No signs, no markings, everything you do is you.
Strangely enough,
Loyalty ... loyalty became critical to me.
Give your word, shake a hand, form a bond,
Stand where you stand.
Where you stand is critical too.
Your value structure defines you.
So, there I was, not yet ten, and learning how to be a man's special friend.
I am not sure what he taught me, but he did teach me that ...
I can only rely on me.
The gift he gave me was I had to become me—
My own me, no one else's me—a me that belonged to only me.
Secrets teach one that there are no rules.
I am not an anarchist, but lines are for fools.
I left home.
I left home so many times.
Before I was seventeen, I left home at least ten times.
Home was not so bad, but there were rules.
I didn't do rules anymore.
At eighteen, I left for good.

I entered the military and started not following rules immediately.
That is what Larry taught me.
If you don't follow the rules … you've got to be good.
That was in 1970, and now it is 2021.
I didn't follow so many rules.
Not following rules should be my legacy.
So, the title of this poem is "What I Can't Do."
Nothing.
Nothing.
There is nothing I can't do!
What I do is totally up to me.

The Tuck

The tuck, my god, what a word.
To a man, this is absurd;
To a girl, one doesn't need to.
To a transgender girl,
The tuck means so much.
I wear skirts, and half the time
It's to cover up I didn't tuck.
Tuck is pain.
Tuck is to physically hide.
No one believes you are a "she."
It isn't about them; it's about what I see.
If I can't buy off on it, why should anyone?
I look down to my new, tight pants and can see.
Not bad, but still a "he."
I bought a "tucker"—the best, supposedly.
Let's just say, it took a week to heal.
I know why this is important to me.
Breasts are the same.
Hair is pretty important too.
The voice, the voice needs to be soft and sweet.
My arms need to be smooth, the nails polished and neat.
I wasn't a girl, and at the same time, I always was.
Every aspect of "girl" was out of reach.
Gender dysphoria:
It's for real.
Every aspect of "girl" is important to me.
The tuck ... the tuck was first.
I was tucking when I was five, I tucked when I was eight,
I tucked all through ten.
When I was alone, no matter what age I was,
I tucked to try to see the girl I wanted to be.
I would tuck, and only me, only me would look.
If I was a real girl, is that what I would see?
I would cry, as I am crying now.
I could never be a girl; what I wanted to see
Would never be.

I have four months before I will never have to tuck anymore.
If all I do is sit with myself …
I want to look down and see something else.
I don't know how to explain
How happy really looking like a girl will make me.

Are My Nipples Large Enough?

I sit here, happy and light,
Thinking about the things that cross my mind.
These are joyous thoughts.
Curiosities.
Are my nipples large enough?
Oh ... please, girl ... I know you know.
It's a topic we are allowed to show.
Yes ... professionally, they are not there.
In the evening, in the evening, they can be there.
What do those nipples say?
Let's settle for "It's cold."
I am not ready to say "I like you."
I am not there yet.
I wish I was.
I am so happy to have breasts.
Nipples will be in my next life.
As a girl, I have never made love to a man.
If this ever happens,
Will he look up and say,
"You have really small nipples"?
Well ... are they large enough?

I Am So Broken

I am so broken.
I am so broken.
I am broken.
I write these poems; I think I am cute.
I am broken.
I am broken and afraid.
Can I rebuild anything worth anything at all?
I think I can.
I am betting everything on that call.
I am walking away from a yesterday
That could have been all of my tomorrows.
I knew that future held nothing for me
Beyond tomorrow; I had to see.
If you are not brave enough to step into your life,
I don't have time to be sad for you.
I wish I did, but I am broken too.
Walk somewhere near.
Some days, walk close, other days, walk far away.
I see courage, I see bravery,
So that my next step is not so alone.
I hope to see you step close to me.
I hope together we can be.
I hope you know what I have to tell you:
If you are too broken, I will have to walk away.
I only thing I have to offer you
Is the courage for you to see me step forward too.
It's too easy to create "being alone."
"Alone" as your comfort zone.
Alone ... alone ... all by itself.
Too much of life is not reality.
Give and take: what a cliché.
The ground beneath you is the ground between you and me.
That is where life feels itself—
Between you and me, and everyone else.
I am not lecturing you;
I am talking to myself.

I need wisdom now more ...
Then I ever did before.
That is why I am ...
Talking to myself.
I am so wrung out now from writing this poem.
I was hoping "Talking to myself" was the last line,
This poem was about being broken.
Can you feel the brokenness in every line?
I am broken.
I confidentially say, "So are you."
Ahh ... that is such an arrogant thing to say.
You are your normal ... please stay that way.
I am broken but in repair.
I am asking so much of everyone around me.
Please let me be a girl.
Please accept me.
Please ... it's OK if you don't understand.
Please be willing to stand next to me.
I promise I won't try to touch you.
Please let me ...
I am broken ...
With you, I can heal.

Point B

As a sailor, I always wanted to sail true to the wind and
course; going most efficiently from point A to point B.

A steady wind is a blessing to a sailor, and
point B arrival has predictability.

No one has a steady wind for their whole life; everyone must
correct their course, and rarely does one arrive ahead of time.

My wanting to be a girl has been a curse; I was
not allowed to sail to my point B.

Being a girl has been my lifelong point B; every
other goal was point C or point D.

All points after point B are points respected by society.

No matter what point course I am on, the point-goals
that all can see, the winds of point B also blow,

knocking me off course, making a course correction necessary.

All my life, the winds of point B blew, sometimes soft, sometimes
a gale; how often in life did I have to trim my sail?

I have a chart table of my life. I keep all my charts there.

Every goal, every shoal, every hazard around which
I must sail; it's all marked on those charts.

Hidden in the chart table is a special drawer with
a secret chart on how to sail to point B.

I have taken that chart out so many times, but only very privately.

A thousand times, I wanted to command, "Set course for point B!"

A life of every course except to point B.

That secret chart is now out, on the table, alone.

I navigate only the course and winds of my lifelong goal: point B.

My story is about surviving a storm that no one else can see.

How many sailors are secretly sailing with the
cross winds of their own point B?

How many sailors are lost at sea?

How many walk a plank of their own design

To find peace finally only after they sink beneath the brine.

This story, my story, is for them: the ones already lost beneath the sea,

But also for the ones still sailing and others yet to set sail.

Without navigational aids,

The ones not yet lost, but soon might be.

A Final Poem to Peter

Thank you for showing me your real.
A hug so soft ... A hug so slow.
I know
I am your friend at arm's length;
Inside that is where I want to be.
Tonight, your hug said, "That will never be."
I can remember how, being as young as you,
Discounting the value of "love for me,"
Nothing could turn me.
I am sure nothing will turn you.
Do you know
Happiness is sharing a dream,
A dream neither of us has ever seen.
Happiness has never been about today.
Happiness is the next moment away.
That is what I see in you.
I hoped you would see that in me too.

You can't ...
I know you can't ...
I was asking too much of you.
I believe in you.
If nothing else, I do.
I tried to tell you why.
Look past the girl in love with you;
See the man that loved you too.
Writing these poems creates so much pain.
I write this one so I can step away.
Thank you for letting me practice being a girl.
I won't ask again for what will never be.

Allow Me to Be

Me, no one else is stopping me.
I need to allow me to be.
Since I decided to become a girl,
I have broken almost every rule.
The rules that are never written down,
But
When you break them,
You
Just maybe
Will be put down.
You know, I don't really care
What you think anymore.
I lived my life
Walking between
Everything you expected of me.
So, basically, I didn't live my life;
I lived something else,
Something that didn't belong to me.
To become a girl, I had to break away.
I had to no longer need your OK.
How does one step away from a life,
A life that got me this far?
My life up to now has given me
The freedom to
Allow me to be
A man wallowing in complacency,
Or maybe
The girl I always wanted to be.
The complacent man … so easy.
The girl …
So much pain, so much hurt, so much undo of my life's work.
The decision to be a girl …
Why can't anyone else see
I am still here; I am still me?
I can never undo sixty-eight years,
But I watch so many undo me, like I was never there.

I watch them through a veil of tears.
I had to step back;
I had to back away from everything.
That was my every day.
Statistically,
No one is going to allow me to be
Anything but what they expect of me.
I am no longer in Iraq; I am no longer in Honduras
Taking care of the poor;
I am not in Bosnia saving people from land mines;
I am home in Maine.
Why do I feel so insecure
Just because I want to be a girl?
Why can't you let me be?
Haven't I given enough?
When am I free of you, all the yous, and you too?
Why do any of you think you own even a little piece of me?
You do.
You don't want to admit it, but you do.
You will allow me to be what you expect of me.
As soon as I stray—
Past Tense: I strayed—
All of you ran away.
I am in Maine,
And I am here to stay.
Unlike you, I am not running away.
Will you allow me to be?
Will you allow me to be?
That is a question you never need to ask of me.

Born Again

Becoming a girl when you're not—
It's like being born again.
To step away from everything you were,
To not be "him" anymore,
To not fight the battles that he fought,
To not evaluate friends on how he thought,
To not get up or, as normal, be crude as any other "he,"
To not buy clothes based solely on utility,
To not lie about that.
Men buy clothes to look like they don't care.
Oh ... they care, but let's not go there.
So, now I am becoming a girl.
So, who do I want to be?
So, so, I told you before:
I use "so" to slowly open a door.
I have to be a whole new me, a me I am yearning to see.
I don't know who I am.
This girl is being built on the ashes of a "he."
I am going to create her very slowly.
Create is the wrong word.
I am going to let her show herself to me.
I don't know how she likes to dress.
How does she reply to slights that hurt, but she is no longer a guy?
Will she be able to sit demure?
What will she do when a man for her opens a door?
The limitations of being a girl—
There are none, but for me ... I would be giving up "girl."
I can never reply as he would.
I can never reply as a strong girl should.
I will be informed I reverted to "he."
So, few will forgive me for giving up "him."
I could say I am sorry,
But I am not.
I have always wanted to be a "girl."
All new, everything ... all new.
What I like and why:

Why I am attracted to another guy?
What I want to do:
How do I wake up next to a lover too?
It's all so, so new.
I have to let myself be born again.
I didn't choose this;
It is what I have to do.
To respect the girl I am going to be,
I first have to let her run free.
I only want to know her.
I am confident that
She will slowly introduce herself to me.

Heart Broken

I had my heart broken by a man.
That is a milestone for me.
He didn't know how I have always loved him so.
Twenty-two years of seeing him and sitting quietly;
I would go to where he worked and sit quietly so as not to interfere.
I did this every week, year after year.
So now, in 2021, I am out as a girl.
Oddly enough, I told him I was out before I told my wife.
I didn't even plan it that way,
It just happened ... It played itself
Months later, I realized what I had done,
So, I went to him and
Confessed my love
I gave him a single red rose, with a little baby's breath.
That was the beginning of the end.
I am a girl;
I know I am,
But I am not a girl for all to see.
For the world around me,
I am a man in a dress.
He has to live in a man's world, and I would want nothing less.
He can't be with me.
That's what he told me
I will never not have been "him."
His friends won't let him be with me.
He wishes he could, I wish he could too.
Too bad the situation made him have to choose.
Buck the expectations of ... are they really friends?
He broke my heart instead.
He broke my heart instead.
He broke my heart instead.

Slightly Drunk

I need to be slightly drunk, so I can cry.
I really need to cry.
Sometimes, I need to cry so bad
I am coming to the end of a "me."
I have to say goodbye.
I have to say goodbye to so ... so much.
I have to say goodbye to everything,
Everything I know.
It's not quite that bad;
The garden outside is still where I will sow
The seeds of my tomorrow.
I will have the same Prius; she is allowing me to keep that.
So, there I will be ... in a Prius as a girl.
I can't yet say ... happily.
So, that is why I need to be slightly drunk:
To say goodbye to so much more than one might know.
I am glad I don't use drugs, because if I did ... I would be on drugs now.
I am hurting so much more than I thought I would.
I am hurting bad.
Now, and every now from now on,
I need to remember how hard it was to be
Not a girl.
It's so stupid, but
Not a girl defined me.
Soon a girl.
Soon a girl I will be.
It doesn't make a difference if I say goodbye.
The goodbye will have been said.
I tried.
I really tried to be happy.
Guess what ... I failed.
I faked happy for so long.
Please,
Please,
Please let me be ... Let me rediscover me.
For a year, maybe more ... I am going to be lost.

I have to know this or I won't survive.
I remember once the knife slipped
And I damn near cut off my finger tip.
That is not what this is about.
How does one cut off everything they are and know?
I don't know;
I think I am going to find out.

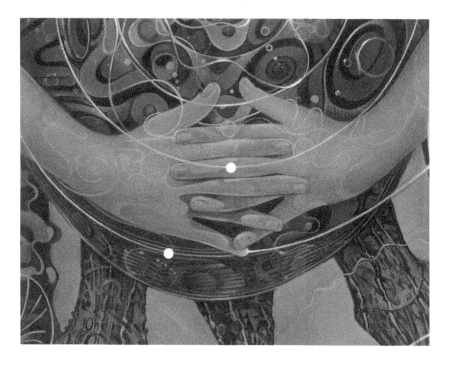

A Girl, Calm and Withdrawn

The doctor asked,
"What is going on?
"You seem so calm and withdrawn."
Normally very engaged.
Tell my story, explain my plight,
Tell of a lifelong fight,
Over a year to explain.
Wanting to be
Something too easy to say.
I was not.
A year.
Reconstruct fragments of memory.
From when I was four, or maybe three,
Up to just a year ago,
I hid.
Very few to know.
Couldn't do it anymore.
Out! Out!
As a girl!
So, I kicked off this whole last year
Explaining myself,
Harboring fear.
Can't get there.
Can't become a girl.
If can't, can't is a final reality.
Where the hell does that leave me?
More than a year,
Passing every test of sincerity
Finally, two letters that say,
"You have permission to try."
I cried the day the courts made me
Legally Lukcia; legally a she.
I cried the day my driver's license also said
"Lukcia ... Female."
I really wish it said "girl."
Yet, there was still more tests;

A critical hurdle, like all the rest.
Medically cleared for surgery:
Cardiology, radiology, hematology too.
If I don't pass even one,
My quest is through.
A call came in just two days ago:
"Everything is good
You're approved for surgery."
So, now I am calm.
I seem withdrawn.
I won the fight that was lifelong;
I am not withdrawn.
I finally don't have to hide whom I want to be,
No longer need to prove my sincerity,
No longer need to prove my body can survive
The upcoming surgical test.
I still could die.
In surgery, there is no guarantee.
So, please understand,
I am not withdrawn.
What you see is the calm
Before the last storm.

I Thought I Would be Nervous

I thought I would be nervous.
I was told so many times that I should be.
I thought I would be apprehensive,
Going forward with fear.
I was told this, too, too many times.
I thought I would change my mind,
Or minimally have regrets.
That is the most common question
Presented to me.
I thought that what I do would make it so I don't fit in.
This was the early warning given to me
By nearly everyone.
I thought that I would have to move away.
I was told so many times that I would need
To move to where there were more of my kind.
I thought so many things.
All of these thoughts were given to me.
None of them were originally mine.
I carry a burden of what is to come.
After a year preparing to be here,
The majority of the burden was put on me
By people who thought they were being kind.
They thought of something, of what, I don't know.
Maybe they thought they were trying to save me
From myself.
They could have thought that what one does
Needs to conform.
Could they have thought selfish thoughts?
They don't want whom I am going to be
Anywhere near them.
Maybe they thought they knew what was best for me.
Maybe they thought they knew me.
I had so many thoughts getting here.
One day away from surgery!
The difficulty in finding myself
Was made much more difficult by

All the thoughts gifted me
By all the people who have no idea.
Early on, I had to learn to wash away these gifted thoughts
So I could see only mine.
I am not nervous now, nor have I ever been,
About what I am about to do.
Now, I was a little nervous that someone would try to keep me
From doing what I am about to do.
Apprehensive and filled with fear?
No.
Of course, I want things to turn out well.
I know what I am asking for;
I was once a surgeon too.
I guess now you know that I am not going to change my mind,
And regrets are for those who don't lead their own lives.
No responsibility for their own mistakes.
I am also not worried about not fitting in
Or
Needing to move away.
I have been a girl in the body of a boy since birth.
I am now sixty-nine,
and
I have never quite fit in,
and
I never moved until I wanted to.
My whole life trained me for this day.
Hi,
I am Lukcia Patricia Sullivan,
And
I am here to stay.

How Can I Not Write a Poem?

How can I not write a poem?
A happy poem,
A poem about being home
After my first surgery—
My first surgery to become a girl.
Facial feminization
Not really necessary;
Needed to support me believing I am finally
Getting to be a girl.
I am in pain, but not more than I thought.
The pain to become a girl is less than the pain to not be.
The swelling will go down in maybe three weeks.
I am riding on a cloud of the girl I might be.
I will accept whatever I get;
Zen-Hope to get what convinces me.
I will have more surgery.
I still dream of the girl I want to be.
I can almost go there right now, but I don't want to.
The girl I see is never called "sir."
The girl I see doesn't spend an hour
Making "him" look like "her."
The girl I see will still be known.
I am not leaving my home of twenty-two years.
Next comes my next *facial en femme*.
Maybe ... Maybe ... I will be a girl,
As if it were nature and not the knife.
Today, I spent an hour with my psychologist friend.
It was one of the first times I spent time with her and didn't cry.
The first surgery is so very huge—
The commitment that can't be undone.
I walked into the flame that I always wanted to walk through.
I didn't blink; I didn't rethink
What it is I want to do.
So, now I wait for surgery two:
Fine-tune *facial en femme*.
That procedure is a month and a half away.

I wish it was yesterday.
How I feel now speaks to me
So clearly; a girl is what I so, so want to be.
Can't explain it;
I have already tried so many times.
If you weren't a boy that wanted to be a girl,
You will never understand.
The best I can do is take care of me,
Finish becoming the girl I always wanted to be.
In three months, I will have "him" physically removed.
In "his" place will be a young lady.
Most readers of this poem may find this …
Something other than healthy.
If you never were whom you wanted to be,
How much does it eat at your soul?
An artist that never had a chance to paint,
A plumber without a wrench to turn,
A child without any support at all,
A boy that wanted to be a girl.
A boy that watched "his" girl life pass "him" by.
A boy that, as a girl in "his" mind, fell in love with other men.
I could go on forever on this weird type of difficulty,
So past caring if anyone understands.
Enough do; their love will carry me.
I am soon to finish this journey.
Remove all, or most, of vestiges of "he."
Someday
Someday, and I hope I live long enough,
I will meet a man that falls in love with me,
And I give him a girl.
I give him me.

Don't Look Up, Don't Look Down, Don't Look Inside to See How You Really Feel

I am watching *Don't Look Up*.
It is really a stressful movie to watch.
How did we get here?
So many don't look inside to see how they really feel.
Is who you are owned by all those around you?
Have your thoughts never belonged to you?
Did you have a thought in a moment you now call "weak,"
Where you were only you?
For a moment, "real,"
No matter how old you are,
You remember that moment that you now conceal.
You folded yourself back into ...
Those around you who think—oh no, not think; they do.
Own you.
I understand fully your distress.
I hid for years wanting to wear a dress.
As Jennifer Finney Boylan once said,
"the bottomless, unfathomable desires that once haunted me."
Everyone has things that haunt them.
Wanting to be a girl has haunted me since age four.
As a teenager, did you watch some asshole rape someone?
Did you fail to come to the aid of a best friend?
Did you go into a store you visited almost every day,
But that time you went to steal?
So many things we do as children,
Windows into our potential real.
It is not a bad idea to learn not to steal,
But I am sure you still would like to.
I still have difficulty confronting a gang.
I usually don't; I grab the girl and try to run away.
The girl too often says she wants to stay.
I have let a few good friends down.

The courage to be a friend, a real best friend;
You have to look inside to see how you really feel.
People don't like going there.
Most gave it up at the age of ten.
Now, our best friend is our brother.
That is what is expected of you.
No ... no ... don't look inside;
Don't look for real.
You just might see someone you spent a lifetime to conceal.
Only you know
The little, tiny pieces of you
That, as a child, were emotionally true.
The vast majority of us walk through life.
Having successfully given you no reason to look twice,
I did it.
I did it until it was real.
I hid the "girl' from everyone but me—
"the bottomless, unfathomable desires that once haunted me."
I am so happy for Jennifer.
She had the courage to break through.
These same desires still haunt me.
I am finally looking inside to see how I really feel.
I am on my way to making that "girl" real.
Unfortunately, I didn't start until I was sixty-eight.
More than a few told me, "It's too late."
I stopped stealing when I was twelve.
I haven't tolerated sexual violence for over fifty years,
But wanting to be a "girl" carried so much more fear.
I am becoming a girl now;
Still have some fear.
I never didn't look inside to see how I really feel.
The only difference now is
I am telling you.

To Have a Chance to Be

To have a chance to be.
What the hell does that mean to me?
What the hell does it mean to you?
A chance to be.
A chance to be.
The goal of everyone who survived age three.
You saw your future and wanted more.
Sitting in a small room,
Little girls and boys learning how to play with toys,
You finally realize.
Realize is pretty advanced at that time,
But you do
Realize that you want:
A chance to be you,
A chance to be …
You realize that you want:
To be something you don't know,
To step into the unknown,
To epitomize a dream gone wrong.
Damn, I hate that word.
Wrong describes nothing more
Than the hate you hold for not-as-you.
A chance to be.
Hopefully, it is more than a lawyer or a priest,
Or anything else between.
A chance to be.
A chance to be.
I still have a chance to be me.
Look hard and long at "a chance to be."
You still have a chance to be
You.

In Fantasy, I Am Soon to be a Girl

Soon to be a girl.
What kind of girl do I want to be?
I would love to love children like my mother did.
I would love to love a man loyally.
I would love to not get broken down by a man's neglect.
I would love to be sensual until in the ground.
I would love to be a woman that more than once goes down.
I would love to not jump ship at that first sign of a better bet.
I would love, from day one, to try to see with sensitivity
Why a man in front of me may be the one.
I would love to not be a whore,
But as a man, I did much more than even that score.
I would love to dress to be pretty, even if only for me.
I would love to wear fishnet stockings, to be the vixen in a fifties movie.
Damn, the challenge ahead of me.
How many things in woman did I see?
I can't do so much of this.
For a man to become a girl is a fantasy.
I am there now.
I am the little girl in the pink dress,
A princess.
Don't tell her or me we can't be a princess.
I am twelve and have a crush on a boy.
I can't tell him; my girlfriends will do that for me.
At thirteen, I start the monthly ritual.
I will never do this, but I was willing to.
I was sixteen,
But no sweet sixteen happened to me.
At seventeen, I joined the military,
And in 1970, it was no place for a girl to be.
As 2021 comes to an end,
So does the person that was "he."
I have no idea how much I will achieve.
All the things I would love to be ...
I don't care.
What do I have, maybe ten years left?

People feigning support say, "You will last at least twenty more."
My ex-wife drove me to my first "become-a-girl" surgery.
She left after she saw me in recovery.
She told me later that as she drove home, she said goodbye to Bern.
Bern is who I used to be.
I know ... I know,
She said goodbye to me,
But she said goodbye to me many years ago.
She just never left the key
For the cage she built for me.
I find it strange she has finally decided to set me free.
Everything she has taken from me all these years
I offered to let her continue to take.
Just give me half the freedom I gave you,
And
Let me be a girl.
I actually know that she doesn't really like me.
I am like a pair of earrings she doesn't like to wear.
An ornament, see! I have an ornamental "he."
I am so glad I have always wanted to be a girl.
A girl ... a girl ... that is what I have always wanted to be.
It's like one of those early love movies:
A man shouts out his love from up high,
His love for a girl.
I am shouting out now,
"I love the girl I am!
I love the girl I am going to be!
I love me!"

Pearls Before Slime

I Am in So Much Pain

I sit here on the cusp—
The cusp of being something I will never be.
I will never be a girl.
Not really.
I keep returning to the concept of
Facsimile.
That is as good as it gets.
It won't get better; I know that now.
I will always be a girl that was a "he."
I have to decide ...
Decide happened long ago.
I didn't know how hard it would be.
This doesn't change my mind.
The wall I have to climb, I will have to climb eternally.
What is wrong with you?
You can't see
Being a girl
Is a good goal too?
I am in so much pain.
As I move into her, the truth comes out.
Everyone I loved, I loved them true;
Everyone I hated, I hated truly also.
So many people can no longer see me.
I walk into a zone of "don't know."
No one any longer seems to know me.
They choose to not know me now,
Because I want to be a girl.
What is wrong with you?
I am in so much pain,
Not because of me.
I am in pain because you can't see past my past.
I don't have time for you.

I am in so much pain,
Because the "you" is almost everyone I knew.
I like being a girl.
This is a gift I gave me.
Give me this gift, please give me this gift.

No Longer Young

I can no longer be young.
So many of my dreams were the dreams of a young me.
Not being young is not just physically.
Fortunately,
Being young is in the mind too.
No matter what I do,
I will never look like the girl that just passed by me.
When I first wanted to be a girl, I was four.
Not as complicated as it was soon to be.
I couldn't navigate
What was ahead for me.
Be "he," be "he"; there is no room for "she."
That is so long in the past.

If It's PTSD, Then Thank You;
It Let Me Become a Girl

Post-traumatic stress:
Can you pass the test?
How low is the bar?
Today, in life, almost everyone can claim PTSD.
I read an article a long time ago,
An article written by *Scientology,*
"Coming through the birth channel is enough
To claim PTSD."
I lived in Clearwater when they took over the hotel.
My brother Jim became a Scientologist as well.
Do you have any idea how soldiers look at that shit?
My immediate society
Has become too explanatory.
This is why I don't fit.
This is why I can't ...
Can't:
The word soldier's reserve.
"Can't" is not part of a soldier's lexicon—
Vocabulary of a person or knowledge.
Your lexicon says everything about you ... The modern man
Never wants go to war; war, is it necessary?
Not a modern man;
A girl now,
Never wanting to go to war again,
Hiding behind a skirt.
Soldiers need help.
They need to give up what made them strong,
That what they can't give up—
Do, did, done.
Did what needed to be done.
Rise up at two, maybe four;
Time means nothing anymore.

Walk into another day.
Does one give up that level of responsibility?
Save you, save brother beside you,
Came to grips with PTSD.
Not a man anymore.
I already proved I can … but no.
Please know:
I really did always want to be a girl.
Unfortunately, it now seems to be an escape hatch.
Maybe … just maybe,
I no longer care.
I have to care about me.
I am going to be OK.
I can always blame it on "Mommy, or Daddy, was too rough."
Didn't you know?
I have always been a powder-puff.
I remember coming back from overseas,
Standing in line at a store,
Listening to people complain about …
Take my word; I had to refrain from …
As I write this poem,
I come to understand my PTSD.
I can no longer accept most of this society.
I am stuck here, though.
Where will I go?
Back to war just to fit in?
The curse of the mercenary.
I think I am better now …
Now—as in "I am a girl."
I am going to blame my being nice.
Let's not stop there; blame politeness too.
How about smiling no matter what?
Being sensitive to you; that's big too.
I am sorry to do that to you cis girls;
I am going to blame being happy,
I am going to blame everything,
On you.
I know I will never be real,

But I really need to be as real as I can be.
I never want to go back to "he."
I won't survive it.
This is the definition of
PTSD.

I Am OK

How do I tell people that I am OK?
I can't go forward any other way.
I want a boyfriend I may never have.
It's more important to want than it is to succeed.
It's more important to see love as its own reward.
It's important to respect the past;
It told me what I had to do.
I had to step away from you.
Only one or two people saw me.
They had to step away in a veil of fear;
I am really glad I am doing this now.
Now ... what is now?
Later is past death.
I am glad I am becoming a girl
While I am still alive.
I have entered the zone where people silently scream,
Stop ... Stop ... We can re-assimilate you!
I don't want to be there.
I never want to be there again.
I will be a girl, silently,
A year, maybe two or three.
I never need to be with anyone ever again.
I don't need you.
You have consistently proven
You are not my friend.
I know already I am going to die alone,
Begging people to understand me.
Don't worry, I am OK.
I saw this future very clearly.
If next year,
I sit somewhere in the woods,
Silently, being a girl,
If I see a squirrel, and because I am a girl,
I find the squirrel cute.
The flowers are bright; I love flowers, and that is alright.
What do I have to do to be a girl in my heart?

It doesn't matter;
I will do what needs to be done.
If nothing else, he taught me that.
I walk away from him.
I am so wrong.
I walk away from him to no longer need to be strong.
I will never be a real girl.
I will never be a real girl.
Do I need to say it again?
No, I don't.
Please make room for me.
Make room for me anyway.
I still want to be in everyone's heart at one point in life.
Were you ever in love with me?
It's OK.
It's OK.
How can I say it any other way?
I doubt you or anyone was ever in love with me.
I am only now learning to love me,
And
I may fail.
Love is so hard.
Love is on the other side of the veil.
If you lift my veil
Slowly ... slowly,
And you see me,
And you see me looking down,
Praying that it's girl you found,
I have no idea what to tell you.
I will silently wait.
I will silently wait.
At the end of silence,
I will be OK.

I Talked with You Today

We came together.
We talked about more than the weather.
You were so sensitive to me.
You knew
I really needed you,
But I couldn't tell you.
You knew and were there for me,
Softly accepting
As
I was trying to express myself.
I am a burden.
I know,
I know.
I put too much on you.
I lost so many, because
Too much was too much,
But
You are still here.
All my friends take turns walking along side of me.
You have no idea how much that—
Yes, that—
Has meant to me.
So, I leave you now.
This poem is near its end.
This poem is the result of learning
Who will walk beside me
As I go through,
Learning to love me.
How does one step into the fringe of their past,
As someone that was always there,
never there at the same time?
How does someone say,
"You knew me;
Now know me still"?
I walk into the future with mostly all-new friends.
It's not my old friends' fault;

They are who they were trained to be.
I love people.
I often have no idea …
OK, I know.
I love them, because a little piece of them
Can see me.
I walk in between two worlds.
Like Jennifer,
I couldn't leave it …
I couldn't leave without loving you as a girl.
A girl.
Don't you know
I want to lay back and let you have
Your way with me?
That type of love is so unique;
It's only occurred
Infinity million times before.
I talked with you today.
You care for me.
I tried to tell you
I am OK,
Because you are here
And
I can talk to you.
You are inside of my pride.
You are inside of my fear.
You are forever inside of me.
You can't stay there, I know.
There is so much of your life that doesn't involve me,
And
I can't mimic you.
I have to become me,
As you became you.
I hope as I become me
I am as generous as you were to me.
Let me tell you now,
As in *now*,
Please listen.
I will never forget you.
I will never forget what you gave me:

The freedom to figure out who I am.
I get ready to go.
I could let my heart write this poem.
Forever,
My heart speaks.
It tells how much love means to me:
Too
Much.
Way too much.
Finally,
Maybe.
Maybe, finally,
I understand love.
Love is a light on the other side of
Pain.

In Bed at Three

I lay in bed.
It's 3:00 a.m.
I have been a man so long.
How can I not be him?
But I want to be a girl.
I want to be a girl so bad.
How do I rectify?
I know that I will never be a girl;
Not really.
I just want to live in that space.
So many people say: OK,
Six foot two,
Over two hundred pounds,
And yet mostly only other girls
Make room for me
To sit somewhere and think
I am here as a girl.
That alone has made a difference to me.
Have you ever wanted to be?
To be?
To be something?
To be someone?
The goal of everyone when young,
It doesn't stop with age.
So many days.
Finally, I am here.
I am a girl at the end of my life .
I really wish I had the time to do
So many things that girls do.
No,
I will have to settle for thinking I am pretty.
Thinking I am pretty will have to do.
I sit on a bar stool
In a club I belong to.
They knew me here
For years before the girl showed up.

It's OK.
I have never been mean.
I tip really well.
They let me be a girl.
They let me believe I am pretty.
Six foot two,
Over two hundred pounds,
Who the hell is kidding who?
Yet, there I am
On the bar stool:
A girl.
Yes, a girl,
Don't forget ...
And happy.

Proud of Me

I am so proud of me.
I am doing something I should have done
So long ago.
I couldn't then.
I couldn't then, year after year.
Now,
I can.
It's like going to college to become an engineer.
I couldn't afford to go to college in '62
Or '72.
Now, I am on the cusp
Of something I have always been.
I always was an engineer,
Building what had to be built,
Creating what didn't exist before
On the skeleton of what always was.
I am here now,
The product of an engineer.
Ah!
A life of work,
To create something
That was not there.
I step into my life now.
I step into my life as an engineer.
What you see,
What you hear,
What ambiance I create,
That's me,
The engineer.
A small break.
Hi ... It's me.
I am still here.
I like who I was above.
It is so hard to be proud sometimes.
Sometimes I think I am living in
A cesspool of pride.

Can you be proud
And cry?
You can
I am a case in point.
I cry.
I cry for what I lost,
For what I had to walk away from.
So many of my tears are sad.
I cannot not see yesterday;
I cannot not see the pain
Of wanting to be an engineer.
Not all my tears are sad.
Years have passed since I knew what I wanted to be,
But here I am,
An engineer at last.
I can't cry *not* sad;
Sad is the curtain of my life.
I cry happy now
Through a veil of sad.
Slowly,
Ever so slowly,
Sad becomes the past.
I am an engineer, a girl at last.

Talking to Someone Other Than Me

Hi, Young Lady,
I sit here at 6:30 a.m.,
writing you.
Guess what?
The objective of the plan
Is flowing right past you.
Every day I wake up and feel slightly different.
My face is different too.
Soon, I go for FFS number two.
A truck ran over a dog in Carmel.
Dover-Foxcroft had extra snow.
Heaven forbids anything happen in Windham.
I don't really care anymore.
I have been through hell,
and
I have so much more hell to go through.
"That was the story,"
I will say.
"Do what you want."
Publish today … Tomorrow … whenever you want.
Never is also OK.
It was never about the surgeries;
It was about several lives being turned upside down.
Ethical conflict.
Your boss is wrong;
There is no conflict here.
I offered you an opportunity to document what is happening to me.
I was a man at sixty-seven, but at sixty-eight, I was a girl.
What does that involve?
How much pain?
How much loss too?
How much cost …
It cost me you.
LGB have no idea how hard the T is.
That was the story.
T.

What does "T" mean?
You missed the point.
I have to go;
You know more about me than me.
Keep it.
I will never ask to undo yesterday.
The third of February, outside,
Maybe Linda is there too.
I am sorry, girl.
If I am there, it won't be with you.
See?
See
What I am going through.
That is the story I want to give you.
I am in so much pain.
I am willing
To walk away from you.
That is the story;
A life-long need,
A haunting of my secret self.
Finally,
Finally, at sixty-eight.
You missed the point;
I am not doing this for me.
I am doing it for the other "mes" out there.
I literally have nothing to gain.
I have so much to lose.
Please stop being driven by your boss, by your ethical ruse.
If this story is not of interest to you
Or the Bangor Daily News,
Just say so.
I wish I was an "L."
That would mean I was already a "girl."
I am happy for you.
I can't explain me.
I can't explain me to you.
I can't explain me to me.
I asked too much when I asked for you to
Figure out how to explain me.

A Hard Time Writing a Poem

I am having a hard time writing a poem now.
I am not crying.
For this poem, crying is not enough.
This poem is about a little girl
Who looked like a little boy.
This poem is not about being seven or eight;
It's about being seventeen,
Forced into the military,
So not ready,
So not ready for anything.
The girl standing there in a barracks with forty other men,
Failing to express, "I am a man,"
I suffered for that.
Grunting, strutting, making unnecessary noise.
That was the currency.
I remember one day I saw a fellow soldier,
Yet more pathetic than me.
He was assigned to sweep the stairs.
In my strange attempt to fit in,
I kicked his trash pile across the floor.
I have never forgotten when I let myself down.
I studied.
I let them know that I could do more than grunt.
So, off to sea.
A quartermaster, and a damn good one,
I was still a girl.
I approached navigation with a certain sensitivity.
How do I tell you what to do as a girl?
Why is it different than what a boy would do?
Emotional investment, I would say.
Maybe I am wrong.
I don't know what a boy would do.
That's it.
A boy that has no idea what a boy would do.
Off to war, just eighteen.
Most aspects of war are obscene.

Literally, in the seventies,
A warzone woman was very rare to see.
It was a man's world.
It was the strongest will prevail.
Two rapes later … I learned to run.
I often was directed to go to a space.
When I got there, a large, hairy rapist was waiting for me.
How do I rectify what happened several times?
I am a girl. Do I actually want this to happen to me?
Maybe … Just not by him.
How do I say I can do this, but only if there is also love?
I am a girl.
For some reason, he could see it clearer than me.
I was raped, unfortunately, more times than two.
Stockholm Syndrome was kicking in.
Did I wish he beat me up yet again?
Did I wish he again threatened to throw me into the sea?
How could I not give in?
These threats were real,
So, before this big fat bastard I would kneel.
I would … and … then I would to … yes,
Until the job was done.
He would dismiss me;
He would only say "Go."
I was always so crushed; I would move away very slow.
I think he liked that.
As I look back,
Rape is about power
Over someone small.
It's amazing I still want to be a girl.
I still actually want to be with a man someday.
Endless hope.
I didn't fantasize being a woman,
I fantasized being a girl.
I didn't fantasize being a lesbian,
I fantasized being with a boyfriend.
Those fantasizes are sixty years old,
But
They are the ones I held.
They are the ones I hold today.

Rape me.
I will stand back up.
Call me a faggot,
Like my father did.
Even threaten to kill me,
As he did too.
It never changed who I was;
It only trained me in how to hide.
If I continue to describe what my life was like,
This poem would be twenty pages more.
I wish I could tell you this poem ends happily.
I don't know that.
I know what I wrote.
I have to stand on that awareness,
Maybe because I finally confessed.
I can look back and see me
As worthy.

Bernard

Bernard sits at the center of my id.
I will never be rid of him.
He wanted to be me as I am now.
He wasn't; he wasn't.
He tried so hard to be the current me,
But he always had to go back to "he."
I can never not be "him."
He fixed tractors, he tilled yards,
He cut down really large trees.
In the spring, he would make sure the beds were ready.
He repaired the cars.
He ordered lumber by design.
To walk away from him,
A walk I cannot take,
To walk away from him is more than a new girl can do.
How do I say, "I loved you"?
I don't want to be you anymore,
But I can never not be you.
Bernard,
I am Lukcia now,
A shell I am learning to step into.
I know who Bernard is.
I know who helped create him.
I now need to be Lukcia.
Lukcia is a girl.
I don't need to be a girl,
I want to be a girl.
Girl.
Say it again.
GIRL.
OK ... I really need to be a girl.
Yes ... something most men never want to be.
Bernard was a man.
How does one escape being a man?
I am so sorry for all the stupid shit I did as a man,
Trying to discover me, and hiding at the same time.

It's 2022, and still I am seen as obscene.
Imagine what 1988 would do to me.
Bernard has to go away;
Becoming Lukcia is not the only way.
Do you know why so many transgender women kill themselves?
Because you wouldn't let them be themselves.
Bernard.
If I was only allowed to be Bernard,
I would already be dead.
That is how powerful wanting to be a girl is.
You don't belong anywhere;
You know where you want to be,
But there is no space there.
Bernard.
Sixty-eight years of wishing I was a girl.
So much unnecessary pain.
Why couldn't I just be a man?
Why did I always feel I was looking through the eyes of a girl?
I have no idea what gender dysphoria is;
I only always wanted to be a girl.

How to be Sad, How to be Glad, How to be You

I am becoming a new me, a me I never saw before.
I will never again see the earlier me.
He is not dead, but he is very much gone.
I now sneak peaks into my new me.
I don't mean to sneak; it just happens that way.
I sit and quietly look and see my legs,
Legs of a girl.
I see my skirt also; I see me as a girl.
I am so far away from him now.
I am sad.
He was a good man; he tried really hard,
He just wasn't me.
So, now I am closer to being me.
I am a girl.
I love skirts and long legs too.
I am sad it took so much pain.
Not the surgeries,
The lifelong pain of wanting to be ...
I now sit in recovery from facial feminization surgery.
It's hard to be ...
You,
Me,
Anyone.
No matter what ...
It's hard to be ...
You might as well be you.
Be sad,
Be glad,
Be everything,
But most of all ...
Be you.

The Truth of What I Do

The truth of what I do,
The truth of what I do.
I lied to you
Almost every day.
No comfort;
I lied to me too.
Where do we go from here?
We ... really only me.
I sit so quietly.
So many hours of ...
Of what ...
Waiting for tomorrow?
A really old, but never a friend,
Told me
I should not display the transgender flag,
Because it might offend someone.
He is a voice;
Only one other voice spoke out.
I have to take his position seriously.
Yesterday is still here.
Bigots still rule the playground.
It's not okay you're queer.
Go somewhere and hide.
Don't share,
Only talk about really soft fluffy stuff.
Thirty-five years have gone by.
Get together and don't be real.
Continue the lie.
Veterinary College classmates reunited,
As if, at one time, we were a team.
Don't you know,
We actually were.
We will never not be of that special group.
I will never not remember you.
I also, never want to see you again.
I remember telling Frank that if he continued to fuck with me,

I would have to kill him.
I still can do that, by the way.
Frank is a narc;
Be careful what you say.
I remember Donna.
Freshmen year, she was only ten feet away.
She smelled of "girl"; she smelled of love.
Such a beautiful person, only ten feet away.
Greg, at one point, took me to his church.
I sat next to him.
There I was, a secret girl, listening to a preacher say
Girls must be obedient.
They must obey!
I had no money.
I was very poor.
I wore the same clothes way too much.
I scooped ice cream as a side job.
I worked at the VA hospital in order to get a free lunch.
I was also in ROTC.
Greg had five parking spaces for his boats and cars.
Five years I applied before I got in;
I had to finish that PhD.
In June, get together,
And know
We were a team.
We were a group of people thrown together for no reason beyond fate.
Don't act like you love anyone;
Act like you respect what we have been through.

To Share the Secrets of a Life

What do you know?
You don't know me.
A thousand secrets I keep silently,
A thousand more are in a box hidden from any view,
And then
A thousand more crushed so deep into the soil beneath my feet,
To find them would require archeology.
I don't want to tell you all my secrets;
It would take too long,
And
It would be unhealthy for both of us.
It's been phenomenally painful to talk to you.
A year-plus of pulling out little pieces of me,
Showing them to you.
I already knew whom I was and whom I wanted to be,
But
You
Helped me see so many of the pieces as sisters.
In the story of my life,
To look at a piece or two,
Even I would find it hard to believe
What I needed to do.
Together, we looked at enough pieces.
Together, the puzzle no longer a guess.

You Want a Reason to Cry?

(Said the Father Who Returned from War)

You want a reason to cry?
I will give you one.
You had a thought that was your own;
That thought belonged to me.
You thought you could be yourself;
You have no idea who you are.
You are who I told you to be.
I gave you freedom to interact with others
Who don't understand.
You don't understand too,
But you know you must comply.
That is good enough for now.
So now, you want to know why you should be allowed to cry.
I cried so hard
The first time I lost a friend in war.
I stopped crying after number three or four.
I sat in the cold beyond the line.
Bastogne was comfort I was too far away from.
Liberated, medevacked, I did not cry.
Life is tough for those who did not die.
The dead are quiet now.
So, I line you up every night to inspect your hands,
To see who has to do dishes and who has to dry.
I sit so many years later now and remember
The court of Mom declaring the crime.
We would lay over the arm of a large chair,
Receive the sting of a belt.
Together we would all silently say,
Don't cry.
Don't cry ... Don't cry.
Don't give him that.
So, now I sit ... I am sixty-nine.
I am only now learning how to cry again.
I can't blame him for who he was.
I also went through a version of hell.

I no longer know who I am,
If I ever did.
I only know that I needed to learn to cry.
I cry for him, I cry for me, I cry for all the sad things that didn't need to be.
Right now, I am trying to be me.
Maybe you are trying to be you.
It doesn't matter;
We all walk toward tomorrow.
CRY.
Yes, I am going to cry.
I am crying now.
How does one walk away from a life so tough
Without tears.
My life has been tears on the edge of my eyelid.
Give me a reason to cry.
Sorry,
Try next year.
I am still me.
I am still here.

Fearful Symmetry

They Don't Understand and They Don't Want To

Gosh ... I have turned my life upside down.
Becoming a girl is so complicated.
One should do this quietly, secretly,
Then move away to be a new self.
Why is there so much shame in being a girl?
Why do men think they own the field;
They set the rules?
Why do girls allow this all to occur
Around them every day?
I am not ashamed to be a girl;
"Being a girl is totally cool!"
Said the man wearing a skirt.
I didn't want to be a boy before I was actually a boy.
I feel terrible that the girl I want to be is a girl from ancient history.
I want to sit and be sweet, to be pretty; at least in my mind.
I don't want to fight anymore.
As a man, I had to fight every day.
So many people learned from me.
I shared my love for being alive
With honor and integrity.
A young boy came to me and asked to learn what I knew
That was more than twenty years ago
That boy is now a man, and he runs the largest slaughterhouse in Maine.
I didn't teach him how to be good, I only showed him the doors
Beyond which his future lie.
I was investigated by the FBI for taking bribes,
Bribes I never took.
How could I help all these people know
What they needed to know
To do what they did naturally?
But could not tell you why the food was safe.
I took them into a tomorrow they were not ready for.
I protected public health by making sure
The food was safe.

I never took a bribe
The girl I am, the girl I have always been,
Took care of them.
They never knew; they still don't know what to think.
Men,
Most men,
Only think of themselves.
They don't give; they don't share.
Men are defined by what they take.
I knew I was a girl so long ago, because
I am defined by what I give.
They never saw the girl that was helping them.
They thought I was just a nicer version of an asshole "him."
So many men define themselves by what they can get away with—
What territory they oversee;
What damage they can inflict.
I am a girl now.
I finally can say that I love people.
I love hard work; I love loyalty.
I love people who believe in themselves.
I love to be part of their family.
So, I am a girl now.
Almost no one understands,
And
They don't want to.
I can say that I think I know me.
I have given myself a gift.
I am a girl, and I will decide what kind of girl I will be.
I decided that I can say, "I love you."
I can say, "I really care."
I can be tender now; I can feel your sorrow with you.
I can now, without words say, "Look at me."
I am pretty.
Now, when I act like your mother; it because a little piece of me is.
I am putting myself through hell
So you can see past him to me, a she.
I am a girl,
But I may never have a man.
Unfortunately, most men can't see past "I was a he."
That's OK.

I just hope I don't end up sitting in my house alone, knitting socks.
I have so much to give.
Maybe I am a girl now just so I can finally give as a girl.
Give, in a manner only a girl can do.
You don't understand,
And
You don't want to.
That's okay;
That is a gift this girl gives to you.

Why Do I Want to Be a Girl?

I don't know.
I don't know what I am doing;
I only know that I have to.
So late to the game,
I still have to do what I am doing.
I wanted to be a little girl.
Back when I was little,
I wanted to sit with the girls
Around whatever they were doing.
As a young lady in my teens—
Oh, wait—I was a boy.
I fell in love with ...
Oddly, I was not allowed to fall ...
I fell still.
I missed my childhood as a girl.
I missed being a girl all through school.
I want to do that now.
I want to be fourteen and have a horrible crush.
Discover skirts and the beauty of long legs.
I want to flirt.
I want to walk gently down a path of girl.
A path of girl:
That is what I never got.
I wanted to slowly grow breasts.
Watch the flower bloom,
Watch the girl I was only in my mind.
I can't go back and relive time.
Every year, I knew what I missed.
I baked pies in the kitchen with my mom.
My family, except my mom, made fun of me;
They always ate the pie.
So much of my pain is not that I want so bad to be a girl;
It was that I never wanted to be a boy.
Being a boy was a curse;
So many expectations that only lead to hurt.
I entered adulthood as a young man,

A role I was never suited for.
I couldn't be a boy.
I had to act as I thought a boy would,
Often taking it to extremes.
The things I did while faking boy are the basis of bad dreams
From when I was twenty to sixty-five.
The girl was hidden deep inside.
My girl came out when I was securely alone;
Even then, I lived in fear.
So, why do I want to be a girl?
Because
I never didn't want to be a girl.
I am not turning this perversion on;
This perversion has always been me.
Why do I want to be a girl?
Because
I *am* a girl.
The perversion is making me be a "he."
How many people have I hurt
Because I was not really a man?
How many promises I couldn't really keep,
Promises made by a false "he"?
I lost so much.
I lost being a young lady.
I never went to a prom, or any dance as a girl.
I didn't do anything as a girl, or a woman.
Nothing as a girlfriend too.
Forty years hiding me from you.
Why do I want to be a girl?
Because I am
Totally late to the game.
Top of the ninth,
And he/she ... what. Who is coming out?
One inning left to make up for all the rest.
She ... OK, she ... Time to call time out.
No time left.
Don't you understand?
There are no time outs anymore.
Why do I want to be a girl?
Because I am a girl—

One who no longer asks permission to be,
One who no longer has time to wait for you.
I am sixty-nine.
I missed out on every age of me.
I would have been a great girl.
Instead,
I was a perverted man.
That's what my wife told me.
She denied me children because I was an inadequate "he."
Why do I want to be a girl?
I want to be the girl I have always been.
Maybe I have ten years to pack all that in.
I don't want to be a boy anymore,
A boy I never wanted to be.
I want to be pink.
I want to be young.
I want so much that will never be.
I no longer need anyone to approve of me.
Why do I want to be a girl?
I no longer want to be a girl.
A girl
I am.
I am now a girl that is ten; I am also a girl that is twenty-two.
I, hopefully, will be a girl on her first date.
I look forward to losing my virginity too.
I am thirty, forty, all the way to sixty.
I am going to do them all:
Blouse too tight,
Skirt to short,
Fishnet stockings pulled down real low …
Go to a party dressed to kill.
What I can't figure out is why …
You all don't want to be a girl too

I Am a Girl Now

Today, I went to a clothing boutique.
I purchased so many real girl's clothes.
I modeled them for the store assistant.
I went into the dressing room so many times.
I came out with a new blouse,
Maybe a new skirt;
I came out new every time.
Waiting to wear these clothes is now my pain.
I just want to go full bore;
Finish becoming a girl.
Today, I finally realized
I am a girl now,
And I can never go back.
As a girl,
How much fun I have day-to-day!
A different blouse,
A different pair of shoes:
So many opportunities to enjoy not only life,
But opportunity to enjoy being you.
Me … in this case, me,
I am a girl now.
I now spend too much time picking out what to wear.
Don't even talk to me about putting on makeup.
All these moments of being a girl type stress—
I love every minute,
Every second of "I am a girl now."
I have come so far in just a little over a year.
I am a girl now.
There is so much freedom in being a girl.
The today girl is no longer defined by a man.
Today girls define themselves.
Well, some, not all.
I am a girl now.
I have dreams of girls;
I walk in a girly way.
My clothes say "woman" to all that see;

I have gentler conversations, it's OK to hear.
I don't know what to tell you, but
I always wanted to be a girl.
I am a girl now.
I no longer need to be accepted,
Because I finally have truly accepted me.
It took so long.
Questions I never needed to ask, but
Were always asked of me?
Nope.
I am a girl now.
I can't wait to see tomorrow how I will dress.
It's joyous to look a different pretty.
I see so many cis women
who don't seem to understand
They dress to look like another man.
Sad.
When I see women that I know worked hard to look
As good as they can be,
I am torn between happy and sad.
Does pretty own them, or is this what they enjoy?
No one else's toy.
I am a girl now.
I already know
That if I ever have a male lover,
They will never own me.
I am a girl now.
Take your time, but eventually understand:
I am a girl now.
I am a girl now.
I am a girl.

A Boy I Never Told I Loved So He Could Stay My Friend

(I Finally Told Him; Now He Won't Talk to Me Either)

I have always wanted to be a girl.
I have always felt mentally and emotionally as a girl.
I have always not been allowed to tell anyone.
Your response is an example of why I kept this secret for sixty years.
I would lay in your bed watching TV with you many, many nights.
I never told you, I never touched you, but that was as close
to being a girlfriend as the secret would allow.
Why do you think I have been your friend all these years?
I am sorry you don't understand;
I never expected anything else.
You can't go there.
Not now.
Not tomorrow.
It doesn't mean I don't love you;
It only means it was the wrong time.
Always the wrong time in your life,
The wrong time in mine.
We didn't fail in loving each other.
I know you loved me as much as you could.
I loved you as much as I could too.
Thirty-plus years ago, men always only friends.
I always wanted to tell you that I loved you.
You know I never could.
How sweet you were to me.
You cared for me as only a best boyfriend could.
I am sorry I challenged your sense of "male"—tough shit, dude.
I was a girl in your bed.
You also never touched me.
How pure can a love be.
I am not afraid of tomorrow.
So many are.
I don't see us ever together again.
Don't worry; I am now old.

The social threat won't last.
I love you.
Guess what, dude!
You can't change that.

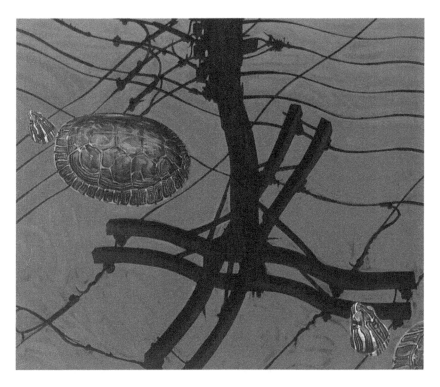

Everything Is Different

I love being a girl.
I reply to waiters differently.
I love being a girl.
I see people through different eyes.
I love being a girl.
I sit up straighter now.
I eat with more constraint.
Transgender girls can proudly exist.
It's so sad,
But it is the key.
Start being proud of being a girl.
Take advantage of everything being a girl can give to you.
That's what a man would do to you.
That is what a man would do.
Do it to yourself.
I love being a girl.
I belong here,
A place I always wanted to be.
Every girl, and now me, needs to stop earning your respect.
I don't care what you think;
You are unaware of how … you … you are.
I am so proud to be a girl.
I survived more than Mom and Dad; I also survived you.
A brother, an uncle, a neighbor that was too …
All the "toos."
I can't risk …
Not being me anymore.
I am a girl,
In my heart,
In my love for life.
It's fun to be slightly submissive to a man.
It's part of what I want to be.
After lovemaking,
After many sighs,
Girls still need to own themselves.
Do we have a word for a man that comes close to equate to "Bitch"?

A word that strikes a girl's soul
And questions gender worth?
No.
Girls need to make one up.
Girls need to say, "You are not acceptable to me."
A man can't be a bitch; that insult belongs to girls.
Damn, I just asked the waiter the male equivalent of "bitch."
Damn, no words effect who they are.
My poems flow.
Normal, based upon my last word.
Being a girl is hard.
It will incrementally improve as girls demand.
Girls need to be in charge of when they make a mistake.
Let them have the high ground; they don't know it's a low version of life.
If they are only a male,
That's okay .
It's nice if a little piece of them is a girl too.
Give them war.
Give them hate.
Give them all the stupid things they can't equate.
Please, girls, never give away your soul, never
give away your ability to love.
Be here,
Be now,
Be in love.
It's not selfish;
It's a life based on true.
I pray for all the girls that still think they are someone else's part-time.
Girls need to be full-time themselves.
I know,
I am working so hard to finally become "me."

Have a Good Cry

I am having a good cry.
Cry for happy,
The courage to be me.
It's so hard.
To look upon your own pathetic self
And still see:
A path to my real me.
The real me is a wisp of thought,
A passing fantasy that is begging to be real.
I spend so much time trying to be my new me.
People tell me I am full of myself,
Yet I am only trying to survive.
I will, don't worry.
I don't know who I am; I have to try to know me,
I meet people I love.
I can't touch them.
I can't hug them.
I am so afraid to become me.
I am stuck between a man and a girl.
I am so afraid.
How can anyone love me?
I don't know who I am.
I don't even know if I love me?
I only know that I have so loved being a girl now.
What happens in the so many tomorrows that are soon to pass?
I have to stop crying now.
I have to take care of myself.
No more poem tonight.
I am so often saying goodbye to myself.

The Secret Life of Turtles

I Am Who I Am

How can I be anyone but me?
So many ... including me,
Become someone else.
I don't want to fit in anymore.
The basic philosophy:
I can't hide anymore.
I walk into a space
I hope you allow.
I want to cry as I write these lines.
Don't you understand?
I can't not be her.
I cannot be he.
Sixty-eight.
Sixty-eight.
God damn it, sixty-eight years!
How late
Can you come to reality
And still survive?
I see myself gone,
Passed,
Nothing left behind.
That's what I try do with these poems.
I don't want to start the war,
But the war needs to be started.
It's time.
Rise up, as I am.
I am a girl now,
I am only going to ask politely.
I am sorry I am not real.
I can never claim "cis."
Do what you want with that.
I don't want to suffer anymore.
Writing this poem presented
So much pain
I had to stop.
To be who I am,

To be who I love—
Hard, Hard, Hard
To be who you can love.
Love.
A minute of love
Is worth eternity.

I Walk Away

I walk away.
I walk away from you.
I walk away from so many yesterdays.
I walk away from me.
No promises to where I go,
Only the promise to walk away.
I walk away to know not where,
Toward no one that I knew.
I can't walk toward a future me;
I don't know where I will be.
I don't know who I will become.
Maybe I have not met me yet.
I only know I am lost.
How to step forward
When forward is no longer clear.
Can't step back;
Everything lost is lost for good.
Nothing to regain,
So now I only step forward.
Forward or behind,
I no longer can see.
I do know that every step I take I am walking away
From you, from me, from everything I knew.
I didn't know how hard it would be
To completely change my life.
I didn't know how many people
Would never again talk to me.
So, I walk away.
I am so past walking back.
There is no back,
There is no past,
Everything is new.
I start again
After one walks away.
One then needs to walk too.
I thought some people would be with me;

No one stayed.
Walk too; I have to walk too.
What is too, where is too?
How do I get there?
I doubt I will ever find "too."
It's OK.
I will never not regret what I have done to me.
I lost everything because people couldn't accept me.
I thought a few would stay with me.
I thought my wife loved me enough.
How wrong could one be.
I walk away.
I walk away from life.

Questions Answered

1. What's it like to be you today?

    There are elements of sadness in my life. This is not sadness because of what I am doing in transition, but sadness due to people who have known me for many years, have known me as a caring and generous person, have known me as one that never really fit in with men, yet were horrified to learn I wanted to be a girl. I know no one of what was my old circle of friends that didn't receive more from me than they ever gave back. A $2,800 custom standup paddle board I purchased for my wife's birthday was reciprocated with a $200 kitchen blender on mine. Every year, for many years, I purchased and prepared hamburgers and hotdogs for many of my wife's mountain-biking social events; no one even once said thanks, not even my wife.

    I could write pages about being taken for granted. Guess what—they don't take me for granted anymore; they don't take me at all.

    So, what is it like to be me today? It's great! I have shed all my false friends, including my wife, and I am no longer trying to please people within which I don't fit in.

    I, me, today: I am a girl. I think I am falling into being a girl better now. I do try to learn to walk like a girl, posture like a girl, talk like a girl, but it is less important now. I am a girl. I am this version of a girl. I do avoid male behaviors that are, and have been, repugnant to me. Maybe that is why I never fit in: I never liked being "dude."

This raises a follow-up question: What's it like to finally *like* me? I wake up and can't wait to be me again. At night, I sleep in really girly, pink pajamas. I spend time deciding what bra to wear and with which blouse. And all of this is becoming my normal. This is good, because I want to be a girl; I don't want to spend the rest of my life *becoming* a girl.

2. What is your level of self-acceptance or comfort in your gender presently?

    During the last two to three weeks—and don't ask me why it took so long, but I dream at night—deep, REM sleep, and I have the most amazing, vivid, full-color, highly detailed dreams. In all these dreams for some time now, I am Lukcia. I am a woman. I told some friends that I now dream as Lukcia, and their response was, "Oh … that's great." Two nights ago, I dreamt I met a man, suddenly I was at my front door with him, and I asked him in. Suddenly again, I was in bed with him. I was on top and he was in me; he was in Lukcia, the woman.

    The dream continued, which was beautiful, because earlier, before Lukcia, dreams with anything near this scenario would wake me up. No, not this time, but no X-rated answers here.

    I woke up and was so happy. I was Lukcia from the beginning to the end. Now I knew: I really *was* Lukcia, at least in my dreams.

3. Are there parts of your life or body that hold you back from feeling affirmed in your gender today?

    I think I am moving past this question. There were parts of both life and body that held me back earlier, with some lingering influence.

In my life, there were so many things I did to be a man that were not me, and that I didn't believe in. There was no other avenue. Sadly, I believe almost all men make up how to be a man as they go, with herd influence predominately in control.

At an early age, I was already actively aware that I wanted to be a girl, but it mostly expressed itself in rejection of the herd values. I started not fitting in before I was five years old. It only got worse from there.

Not caring what others think is the freedom I now experience— "others" being all the people of my past. Today, for the most part, I no longer use most anyone as a window into who I am or an indication of my value. I already did this for most of my life, but not to the degree that set me free. I am free now.

The part of my life that held me back mostly was that I hated how men were; I hated how they interacted, how manhood was an echo-chamber of values without anything I could respect. I look back now, and even much earlier, and see them just as lost as me. Someone set the standard, and the others followed. That was my failing; I would contest the alpha male. I would "out-dude" him, "out-crude" him, out … damn near everything.

I was a leader all my life, but a girl inside. I never liked a man that wasn't nice; all the rest can go to hell.

I couldn't roll over and be a girl; only girls could get away with that. I told a few about my real self, and they never talked to me again.

I don't regret hiding myself for so long. If I'd come out in 1973, I would probably have been in a grave long before now. The part of my life that held me back the most was the years and years of training in how to hide—which I failed at, by the way. The hardest part was overcoming a life of being told, "Don't be yourself."

I am so new to being me.

My body …
I have arranged to have this addressed.
Soon, the offending parts will be gone.
I no longer need to pull them as if to rip them off.
No longer need to bind them tight.
To me …
A bad vagina is a better sight.

I actually don't need a vagina …
I just need them gone.

I also wish I didn't have a beer belly.

4. Are there parts of your life or body that bring you joy?

Difficult question.

Most of my joys are still quite private.

I look at myself in the mirror. I see Lukcia. *Yeah!*

I put on girl panties, and they fit.

I have fake tits that are forever firm; I still wear a bra every day.

I sit with a man, and I hold the presentation: soft voice, a little flirting, a little playing with my hair—perhaps too much.

My life and body, for now, are the same thing.

5. How do you navigate and cope with the experience of misgendering, discrimination, or microaggressions?

   I don't do discrimination or microaggressions; I personally think that it too late for them. I let it pass and simply avoid the source.

   Misgendering: I am okay with that. I do it to myself. I politely and softly tell them I am a girl, and the term to use is miss. The vast majority of people immediately apologize. My gas station attendant kept calling me "*sir.*" I finally told him that I have been a girl for over a year, and my title is "miss." I informed him that I have been a good customer at that full-service station for over twenty years, and he gets it right or he loses my business. He calls me miss now, I buy his gas, and he even washes my window.

6. How has your understanding and presentation of your gender evolved over time?

   I no longer care to anywhere near the degree I did. Now I forgive myself for a slightly male voice or gesture. I don't let anything stop me from "flowing into" myself as a girl.

   I am very sure many people that have known me for ten to twenty years think I am totally nuts. I don't get down and become my old self for them; no, they never earned that from me.

   I am Lukcia.

   The difference now is that I believe it.

7. Describe who comes to mind when you think about receiving support.

   My sister Debbie, and a girl friend named Jamie.

The Papillon Center and the staff—that is actually their job, but I think them sincere.

Audrey, the softest touch of consistent support that has always been there for me.

You.

8. What have your experiences with medical professionals been like so far in gender affirming care?

The Woman's Health Center was clinical, but professional and supportive.

My primary care physician was and is afraid of me, but he stoically sits up straight as he supports me. He always has a female doctor in the room with him and me.

It's all good.

9. What is a wish and a worry about this surgery?

I stopped wishing and worrying some time ago … ago … ago. Now it is only "GO."

I do want a functional vagina. I want to make love with a man. If I can't make love, I will eventually settle for sex. D. H. Lawrence said it best: "Love is on the threshold; all animals have sex."

I will never hurt myself, but I am not afraid to die. My life has been hard; I will not cry when I say goodbye. I believe I was significantly autistic as a child. In college, I volunteered to babysit an autistic child so the parents might get some time away. This required some training in autism. As I learned the signs of significant autism, I saw myself: non-verbal for years, repetitive motion behavior, expressionless staring as people attempt to talk to me, very internalized in thought. I could then, and can still, be in a social situation with a group, and yet not be there at all.

I never learned small talk. I didn't talk almost at all until I was six or seven years old. After that, I rarely talked. About sixth or seventh grade, I finally started to assimilate knowledge. Prior to then, I was the worse student to ever get promoted to the next grade. I did first grade twice. I completely skipped fifth grade. My parents took me out of Catholic school and put me into a public school. Shortly after that, they took me out of public school. My father kept me with him for the remainder of that school year.

Autism and gentle social banter don't mix well. With time, I could talk with people in a social setting, but my contribution was always about some piece of knowledge I learned. Historically, I was never invited to parties as an individual, only as Emmy's husband. I lectured some knowledge; I demonstrated an informed person's take on science and government. I love to teach, but at a party, people didn't go to learn.

Long answer: I wish that as Lukcia, the Lukcia with a vagina, I will finally have small talk, easy type discussions, like how much I love scarves, fashion accessories, or how to dress with color and balance. I have never been able to do this, but I believe Lukcia is already doing this. Topics that are not knowledge, not objective or factual, topics that are soft and subjective where no one is wrong, everyone is right.

Maybe I will be invited to parties.

10. How do you envision experiencing your body or life after having this surgery? How do you expect this surgery will shift how you see yourself, how others perceive or relate to you?

I have already shifted in how I see myself; as about others' perception of me or relation to me: I don't and can't give a damn.

The surgery will allow me to feel that I did everything I could to be a girl. I will not fail for lack of trying, for lack of want, or expense.

I really feel like I am a girl now, even prior to the surgery; I still need the surgery, I still need to complete the … whatever "complete the" is.

I will never be real. I will only be as real as I can be.

There is not much more I can do; the rest is up to all the other yous.

11. Who can you turn to if you are having a hard time and need emotional support before or after surgery?

True support. True understanding.
Audrey, you, and my sister Debbie.

I have my had to be the primary support person of myself my entire life. The natural power of my darn near fearless decision-making has been my support. Hundreds of major decisions made alone, made crisply, made with full responsibility for the decision. I turn inward, I seek advice from the one person that actually knows me: *me*.

12. Can you identify other emotions you feel when thinking about this surgery or the intended results?

Yes.

It will be the true and final ending of Bernard. I will be sad at this not-quite total loss. He was actually a very nice person, but I am happy in that I believe the better parts of him are still here in Lukcia. Maybe being Lukcia is my way to escape the bad habits of Bernard, to reject all the rejection I experienced throughout life. I am still being rejected, but as Lukcia, at least I am having fun.

It's difficult to explain how much healthier I would have been if my male genitals were gone sixty years ago. I didn't like them even prior to puberty, but it became obsessive after puberty.

I very emotionally wish I had done this so many years ago. It's not too late, but damn near.

Here is a new set of questions you're invited to reflect on:

1. How is your inner child, Little Lukcia, doing these days? What brings her joy? What scares her? What comforts her? How old is she? What's it like to think of her and be with her?

    Lukcia has fluid or dynamic age associations. Depending on what I am doing, I can be almost any age of a girl at least past puberty. I find joy in little things that only a young girl would find joy in, like a new, sexy bra, or totally awesome panties. The situation and the visuals are that of a young girl. When I wear a short and revealing skirt, I dance around and wiggle like a young lady discovering herself and the joy of being herself. When I put on a long evening dress and have nice necklaces and my hair is just so, I walk with a certain mature pride that I equate as a girl of thirty or all the way to sixty-nine.

Most everything brings Lukcia joy. I have years of discovery ahead, years of experiencing life as a girl—old or young, but still so new. Lukcia is only afraid of mean men that are willing to hurt her for almost no reason at all.

I am Lukcia, but I will keep answering in third person because I am flowing. Lukcia finds comfort in knowing people that accept me, and some even like me.

It is very nice to think of Lukcia, because I made her up, and I make her up a little bit more every day. I make her as I discover her in me, as I find how I want to be as a girl, discover my new value structures. I am very close, so there is no being with her. Lukcia and all her newfound values and wants, her dreams of a desired future; these things are all inside of me without reference to my name. Becoming Lukcia has allowed that hidden girl to slowly leak out. Lukcia is not going to fuse with Bernard; Lukcia is close to totally replacing Bernard. Some shared values may remain, but I will be all Lukcia. I actually feel as if I have done this already. I rarely sense him anymore.

2. Can you think of a moment (even a micromoment) when you experienced touch that felt safe, warm, friendly, and welcoming? It might have been self-touch (running your hands through your hair, or placing your hand to your heart) or touch from another person. What did that feel like? What does it feel like now to remember it?

A young man I have known for twenty-plus years informed me how much he accepted me as a girl, and then a few days later he asked me out. We would meet for a beer or two, and then we would go to dinner at a nice restaurant. On our third date, we were sitting across from each other, and he reached across to take both my hands in his. His movement was slow and deliberate, his touch was soft and caressing, as he gently held both my hands and cupped them in his. We sat there together for a few minutes, just both of us looking at our hands together. Then he slowly and respectfully let my hands slide out of his.

I felt respected as a girl; I felt accepted as a girl. I felt so light and in shock as to how beautiful it was to experience a few moments of my lifelong goal of being a girl to feel so good.

It still gives me goose bumps to think of those few moments. His friends and coworkers gave him a hard time about dating me. He dropped me, and we don't see each other anymore. He gave me a gift during those few moments: I, for a few moments, really was the girl in a relationship of mutual love and respect. That moment set my standard of the kind of relationship I want to someday have.

3. Can you think of a place (real or imagined) that brings you a feeling of freedom, joy, peace, safety, or comfort? Try going there in your mind, and notice your surroundings. Are you in nature or indoors? Are there people there or are you in peaceful solitude? What does this place look like? Really take a look around and name things you see. Do you notice any smells, sounds, tastes, or tactile sensations? Is there a word that describes this place? Try going there in your mind from time to time to just be, or to say that word to yourself to bring up that feeling.

Almost all the places that bring me a feeling of freedom, joy, peace, safety, or comfort are real places. The earliest and still most common one is in my house, alone. I dress up, or I spend an hour doing makeup training, or I go through my clothes putting on different groupings of skirts and blouses. I often find myself doing what I call my "happy girl dance." I swirl, I twist, I exaggerate my hips, I flip my hair, and I laugh at myself.

The next real place is when I am with my sister Debbie. She touches me, she hugs me, she kisses me like a long-lost sister. It was so easy to relax into her generosity of love.

The next place is in my dreams—some fully asleep, some in twilight. This took some time to become the inviting place it is now, but it always was nice. In these dreams, everything is lighter—not too bright, but light enough for me to see everything. Everything is tactile, and yet all is soft and gentle. Everything is emotion laid; emotions of joy and discovery, of in-dreams moments of self-awareness.

The sounds are there, but they are nonintrusive in nature, indistinct in nature upon my awakening. The sounds are very soft and gentle in their support of the dream. That is all I remember of them.

Taste I've experienced only once so far, in a dream when I was with a man. I tasted him.

I don't have a single word for each and every one of these places. I have three words that recapture for me the two that involve only me; one place in my house, and the second in my dreams: "Girl-In-Love".

Girl-In-Love with being a girl, with a pretty skirt, with a special dance of joy. Girl-In-Love with the thought of a man, of a soft touch, of a dream so real it almost satisfies my needs.

Girl in Love

I am relaxing into myself now.
I have shed apprehension of what is to come.
What is to come is here.
I stepped through fear;
I stepped through hate.
I stepped through the veil that makes everything unknown.
I know now.
So many as me say they always knew.
I said that too.
So easy to say before one changes course
And sails to a long-sought destiny.
I entered the fog of freshly coming out.
Oh, so proud, and my commitment shining anew.
Then the challenges of every day:
Every "tut", every *looks away*.
Months and months,
Told to question myself.
So many nights crying myself to sleep,
Steeling myself for the next day.
I revisit the thousand times over sixty-seven years,
Praying to be a girl.
When I visit my early self,
I know
Friends fall away.
Wife leaves.
I shed them or they shed me.
Away they seemed to fall from me.
Slowly, Bernard seemed to fall away too.
A girl remained,
Like a flower stem that no longer bends to the wind,
A bloom yet opened.
A young girl, unformed, but a girl.
I no longer love or hate Bernard.
He's not anywhere to love or hate.
Learning all anew to love myself,
Girl in love.

Girl in love with being,
So beautiful to feel that special goal inside
The warmth of love so truly felt.
Inside,
All by itself, all for itself.
Girl in love,
Relax into my discovered love.
Soon, my love is leaking out.
I love the sky, I love the sun,
I love little birds and woodpeckers too.
I love the person that was my wife.
My love says "Go … Be happy too."
I relax into myself.
Girl in love.
I love pink, painted my bedroom pink
To match my panties and so much else.
I loved slowly growing breasts.
I loved actually needing to wear a bra.
I shave my legs twice a week,
And I love it.
The wind tingles my legs.
The bed sheets caress me.
The joyous difficulty of figuring out what to wear …
Girl in love.
Now, I am a girl, fluid in what age I want to be.
In a short skirt, I feel so young and pretty.
An evening gown makes me feel mature and beautiful.
I am a girl in love with being me.
So much to learn, so many challenges ahead.
I love the path before me.
There is no fear, there is no hate
That I pay attention to
There is only a girl in love.

What Happens When You
Finally Don't Care What
Others Think of You

I always wished I didn't care what others thought.
One gets so wound up in wanting something not fully understood.
I always wanted to share, even if only my time sitting close to another.
Since birth I was never truly a member of any definable group.
Always on the edge of belonging,
I was nonverbal, or nearly so, for so many years.
I still wanted to be slightly in the aura of some group.
Years it took to learn that I had to mimic a group to belong.
I could fake the group's personality, but only to a
degree still insufficient to truly belong.
So many groups throughout my life allowed me to exist on the fringe.

Goodbye, Mom

I said goodbye to Mom today.
I said "Mom, I have to go"
I know I am a young girl,
But
I need to become a woman now.
Mom,
I remember when I first told you
I want to a girl be.
You took me under not your care;
You took me under your love.
I was new to being a girl.
At the most, I was twelve or thirteen—
A child to all I wanted to be.
You taught me how to grow up.
Slowly.
I wanted to move so fast—
A child to a woman
Overnight.
But, Mom, you walked me slowly.
Our talks were with depth I never felt before
But never more than I could bite.
You learned of me as I told you of my dreams.
You walked through my dreams with me.
Soon I was a girl,
No longer a child.
A woman was still a distant quest.
I tried to say goodbye.
That is what all girls must say.
To a woman be.
I was a female child;
A girl I became.
I don't even know how you did it.
You didn't tell me
How to step
Or
Where to step

Into my life.
You were the gentlest mother.
I always felt okay moving forward,
You by my side.
I felt cared for
Through twelve and thirteen,
Through puberty,
Through impending womanhood.
You always there beside me
As I learned
I am a woman now.
I told you goodbye to be free;
I will never be free of your gentle love.
You will always be my mother,
No matter how independent I seek to be.
I can't say goodbye.
I really should have said,
Please,
Let me
Try
To walk alone.
I know now;
To walk as a woman
With pride
Was all you wanted for me.
Gentle love.
So,
Gentle love
I give to you.
I am Lukcia.
I am your daughter.
I love you.

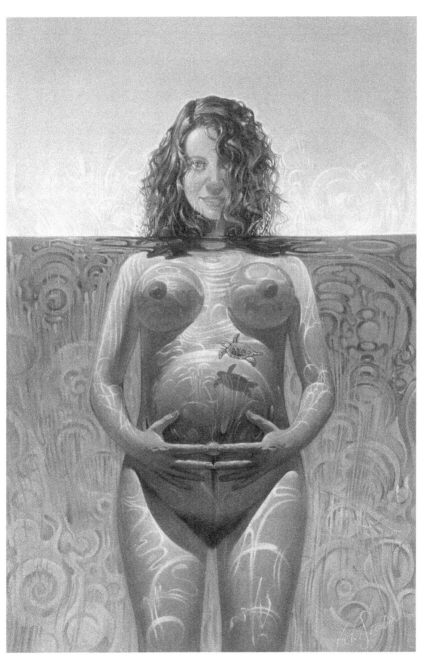

My Madonna

Gender Euphoria

How to say how happy I am …
It's hard to describe.
It's so different than every other happiness I ever had.
I feel a calmness in my heart and soul.
I am no longer a "he"; I am a "she."
Wanting to be a girl is a double-edged sword.
I didn't want to be "him" anymore—
Actually, never did.
I always wanted to be a girl.
I had my vaginoplasty surgery six weeks ago.
The Doctor removed "him" from my view.
Now I see a girl down there.
Gender euphoria:
I don't have to be "him" anymore.
The value structure I had to live within is gone.
I look down and see "her."
She is there; she is there,
Right between my legs—a girl.
I feel complete; not maybe a girl, but a *girl*.
I wear tight pants that smoothly curve around my groin.
There is no "maybe something is there."
So many years of tucking "him" away.
So, for a short while, I could fantasize I was a girl:
Short skirts, tights, and leggings all now look as only a girl could be.
I now can go to the gym and enter the girl's room confidently.
Confronted: I will prevail!
Even if I have to show them my young lady,
Gender euphoria includes the promise of sex.
I can have a boyfriend now;
I can be a female for that man.
I feel liberated from the sense of being "gay."
I never was truly gay.
I can approach a man and know that, if it happens,
I am offering him a girl
The euphoria of that now-opened door,
All because I now have a functional vagina—

And don't forget: no penis or balls.
I am now free to be a sensual woman,
A woman that can follow through.
I never have to explain him again,
How to explain a dream come true.
How to finally be a girl, yet so late in life,
I couldn't go halfway.
Live a lie for so many years.
Finally, I am true.
That is gender euphoria to me.
I put on really nice panties.
I look down and cry.

Quieting Down

My vagina is finally relaxing,
Letting me attempt to accept her for what she is.
I am a girl now ... that's what all the doctors say.
I am not a girl.
I am an old man trying very hard to be a girl.
I will never take back what I have done.
Wanting to be a girl is to want to live the life of a girl.
I just want to be not him anymore.
I missed girl by sixty years,
But that was the dream.
Now, I get to be a girl and a fool at the same time.
I worked hard to be able to afford to be a fool.
Being a girl may cost me more.
I never cared about being the fool.
Being a girl has not cost me too much yet.
I will never be a girl; sixty-eight years a man can't be undone.
I will forever be an old man trying so hard to be a girl.
I won't turn back.
I can't turn back.
Give me ten years as a girl; go along with the joke.
Let me be a girl.
I promise I won't hurt you.

Hi, Timmie

Hi, Timmie,

Your ex-wife has it right. It takes time for others to accept you
as the new you. As I am, the new you is so close to the old you
that you wonder about the social rejection by old friends. Some
friends will immediately accept you, while others may take weeks,
months, years, or eternity. Some will immediately accept you
over the phone during the pandemic, but upon seeing you for the
first time, withdraw from you; this happened to me recently.

It is with a generous heart that you need to let everyone find
their own response to you, allow that response to mature,
and hope the friendship returns. Try to remember the gift
you gave yourself when you finally said, "I am a girl!"

For me, that moment was very hard, not because I didn't already
know that I have been a girl at heart all my life. It was difficult for
me to speak these words out loud, knowing that I must now speak
them out loud publicly. I only spent sixty-four years coming to grips
with who I always wanted to be; can anyone else be any different?

We all live in a shell that is the outward expression of ourselves—
that which is radiating from our own heart and soul, and how that
personal radiation combines and mixes with the radiation generated
by all others. This mixing is the "social construct": the unspoken
expectations of others now in conflict with your new brilliant light (I
can see you are radiating beautiful, brilliant light; shine on, girl!).

Everyone wants you to stay the course, act tomorrow as they expect
today that you will act tomorrow. Predictable social interactions
allow people an easy comfort in the relationship. I, and you, took
that away from our social circle, family and friends. They most likely
still trust you. Maybe not, but they most assuredly have diminished
trust in their knowledge of you, what their social expectations
of you are or should be, and how when both of your personal
radiations co-mingle what will be the resultant illumination.

So yes, your ex is right. Time will let those old friends that can adjust slowly return to your social circle, and it will fail also. Most people live locked into a social construct that is predominately built by those around them. These people don't own themselves; they are owned by others. When you came out, you made one *very powerful* statement! You said to the world, "I own me!"

Time will also allow new people to see the new you radiating from within. There will be those who are intrigued, curious, willing to learn, and want to feel the warmth of your special light. These people will be your new community. There is a reason why the social circle of transgender people is other transgender people.

That is what is so beautiful about the transgender community; it is made up of people that are attempting to own themselves. Every one of us is somewhere along the path to self-actualization. Do you have any idea how many people can't do this?

In conclusion, take your time to learn to own yourself. Live your life day-to-day, but soon live *it* also week-to-week, then month-to-month, etc., until you are fully living your life. A life you own!

Love,
Lukcia Patricia Sullivan

Love Learned Silently

I watched a man—

A boy; let's not forget that what I watched was a boy.

I approached and watched; of course, silently, because silent was all I was.

Being next to Mom wouldn't do anymore;

I had to go outside and do "boy" things.

I would walk hours in the woods; silently, slowly stepping to anywhere.

I came upon a farm across a field.

I approached and watched; of course, silently, because silent was all I was.

Forty years later I would do this as a soldier, but
that day, I was a creature without alliance.

Not a boy, not a girl, not a son, not a brother, not a friend:

The silent "not."

I entered the barn as a spy; a skill honed by my life at home.

So many skills developed as a child to survive.

I left in spy retreat to silently step slowly home.

No one ever questioned where I had been, or why
I was ... For me there was no early or late.

Ten years old and the cast was set: silenced into
not being the many available things to be.

Prior to this: going to Grandma's house every summer for the summer,

Too not-integrated to know that the rest of the
family spent the summer at the beach.

Grandma told me to wet the bed all I want, it didn't matter.

I stopped wetting the bed.

Grandma died when I was ten; I started wetting my bed again.

Just like that old movie of the Olympic runner; I, too, would find
myself at four or five in the morning, running around the side
yard, holding my bed sheet high, trying to dry out the pee.

I was the only child in the house with their own
bedroom because of the stink of pee.

I came upon a farm across a field.

I approached and watched; of course, silently, because silent was all I was.

I met some boys slightly younger ... slightly
older than me ... slightly like me.

I walked out of the woods, and they embraced
me as naturally as wind or rain.

They were my first real teachers in life.

They shared who they were.

Get the cows in, close the stocks, shovel the
silage, and give them the grain.

Day after day, I did, and did again; never better, never worse, just did.

I was never treated as an equal; I was treated as
someone that showed up for work.

I learned the cows; I learned to move gently between the girls.

I worked every day at that farm for three months before Mr. Henry Camp came to me and said, "OK … thirty-five cents per hour."

He knew I would work for free, but he knew I needed to grow. All the other boys were "state kids," where this was their most stable home.

Little did they know, it was also mine.

Sometime later, an older boy showed up, and he bullied everyone.

Long story, but he got into a fight with Opie, a much smaller boy.

This is where I watched a boy.

The fight didn't last long; Opie was pinned down with his arms to his side, the bully sitting on his chest.

As all the other boys watched, the bully took out his penis and made Opie suck it.

I watched for a minute, maybe two, in disbelief.

I stepped over and knocked the bully off of Opie and said, "Now you are fighting me."

I went blind, I went blank, I went … and then went again.

Sometime later, the other boys were pulling me off the bully; something they didn't do for Opie.

I had the bully in a cow stock, head locked down, and I was just hammering him.

Opie was safe but violated, the bully was Henry Camp's nephew; he went home, and I was in an unfamiliar zone.

A few weeks later, Henry Camp got me another job at the Albright's farm at one dollar per hour.

I never got better at belonging than I did with those state kids.

They lived a life of "not-belonging."

They, and I, belonged to "not-belonging."

There they were, as was I.

"Not-belonging" as a lifestyle, a lifestyle of sliding in
between … in between all of life's "tweens."

I was eleven … fifty-nine years ago; I still don't
belong anywhere in particular.

Too many people acted like a friend only when
they wanted something from me.

I am not so many things.

Many of the things I am make others uncomfortable.

I approached life and watched; of course,
silently because silent was all I was.

I met some men, some slightly younger … some
slightly older … some slightly like me.

I walked into life, and they didn't embrace me
with kind winds and gentle rains.

They were my second real teachers in life.

They shared who they were.

Fifty-nine years ago, I already learned

I may never belong, but I will, as many others won't …

I will show up for work, I will step up too … stepping up defines who one is.

I am no longer a boy … Now, I am a girl.

I, oh, let's say "suffer" the indignities of laughs and sneers, the waitress that can't seem to have time to take my order, the group of cis girls that poorly hide their curious peeks at the freak, the really crude man at another table that calls me a "faggot" three times.

It hurts. It hurts a lot, and yet, it hurts not at all. I spent a life being trained in not-belonging, so I am prepared.

Long ago, I decided I can't spend a life being an unloving person.

I already knew I was a girl at heart and soul.

I am going to love, even if another can't.

I sit in a restaurant I frequent. I always tip well; I am always polite.

A waitress I know well walks by, and I say hello.

She is off-duty … she turns … looks … turns away … she doesn't have to be tolerant; not now … she is off-duty.

Love is something you give.

If you expect anything in return … it isn't love.

Return is nice.

Love is a pure gift … the purest gift of all … Give love.

I will return to that restaurant again … and again … and many others.

The Zen of Love is all.

Love all that appear unworthy of love, as you would love that which appears blessed with worthiness.

I strain to see your "now", as I strain to see my own "now."

I barely comprehend my "was", so much of my "was" is told in lies.

You're "was": an incomprehensible complexity of
"you" and "is", mixed with yesterday.

To judge is to give up the gift of giving love.

"Yet to be" for everything from pebbles to both of us is a toss-up.

Most likely everything and everyone will end up washed up on
the beach rubbed to smoothness from the surging surf of life.

Beach glass ...

The Zen of Love is pretty simple: Love everything

Love every piece of beach glass; no matter how soft
or rough the surf that made it smooth.

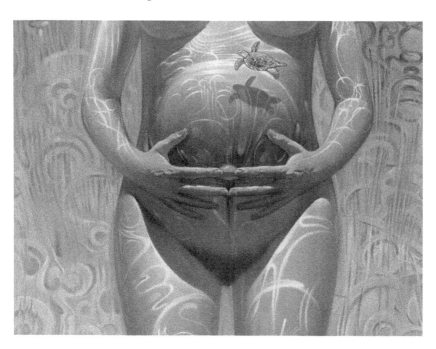

You Can't Not Be

You can't not be a man,
You can't not be a boy,
You can't not be everything you were.
You are only, and will ever be the culmination ...
You ...
You is me now.
I speak to you all.
We can never see or hear that which culminated us here.
You ...
I expect nothing from you.
These words are of you, too, the not me.
A culmination.
Me ... yes, me now!
I am culminating all that I have been and wish to be.
I have wanted to be a girl for so long now,
But what does that mean?
How does one culminate a dream?
How to culminate a life not allowed?
Culminate ... where am I ...?
Culminate into an every night cry:
"I am a girl now!"
What does "now" mean?
I can go into a large store's woman's room,
Confronted, drop my pants.
That is not the girl I wanted to be.
I wanted to be a girl.
I wanted to be a girl in my heart.
I wanted to be the girl I always have been.
I can show you now,
Something I never wanted to show anyone.
I can show you that I am a girl,
So that your mind can see.
"You can't not be."
I can't not be.
I was a boy,
I was a young man,

So late in life I decide to confront you.
No …
I confront me …
I am a girl.
I am a girl, and I want to be a girl.
I have done and will do everything necessary to be a girl.
Everything necessary … what does that mean?
I lost control of my own definition.
So many months now … so much pain,
So many dollars spent to satisfy who?
Yes, I needed it to satisfy my fear.
I always was who I was, yet unaccepted.
Did anyone cause me to be inadequate?
Why did I accept this inadequacy?
"You can't not be."
I can't not be everything I was.
I have a vagina now.
Is it for you, or for me?
I know now that it is the step away.
It is for me now.
I step away from
Him,
History that owns me,
Who owns who owns who owns who …
I can't not be.
Everything I have ever been,
I know … I know so deeply;
I have always been a girl.

I Stand at Night

I stand at night,
But who does stand there?
The man that braved a conflicted life?
Someone who walked through pain so many times?
Am I standing there as the girl I now am?
Can I ever truly be free of him,
His skill to survive?
I stand there ... in pain.
My new vagina needs so much care.
Only he can bare this much pain and challenge.
She is so young and is lost as to who she is.
I stand in pain.
I look down and see her.
I know that
He is why I have the strength to be her.
I can't leave him yet;
I need him so much now.
His courage is the courage I need to walk away from.
She ... my new me,
Doesn't want to be courageous anymore.
I want to only be.
Please.
Please.
Let me.

I Am a Girl

I am a girl.
I don't know how to explain it to you more clearly than I already have.
Maybe I didn't do such a good job.
Maybe saying, "I have always wanted to be a girl" wasn't enough.

In reality, I didn't always want to be a girl.
In reality, I always *was* a girl.
You couldn't see her,
But her boy was literally only skin deep.

I initially didn't understand that I was not a girl at age four.
Telling me I was not a girl didn't make me not a girl.
Punishing me as I presented as a girl
Didn't make me not a girl.

I did girl things;
I did not do boy things.
At no age did I seek to do boy things.
My skin was a lie that all preferred to believe.

My childhood friends who were girls
Abandoned me at their change in life.
At age thirteen, I started wearing Kotex in
my pants for three days a month.
It didn't work … It didn't make my skin stop the lie.

At age twenty, I was in love with a man,
A man I never touched, but spent every day with for months.
I told him that in truth I was a girl, and I wanted to be his girlfriend.
I got one hug in before he never talked to me again.

This attempt at love as a girl was tried twice more.
The same results prevailed:
The lie the skin professed overpowered
The sensitive, loving girl that was really there.

No, I didn't always want to be a girl.
I always was a girl.
My caring, my love of others, my wanting a boyfriend,
Everything I was, was the girl hidden by the skin's lie.

I am a girl.
I have altered the skin's ability to lie.
There is only so much one can do;
The skin's lie is now a whisper, but not gone.

I am a girl.
I want to feel love with a man,
As I have attempted to do in the past.
Will anyone get past the skin's whispered lie?

I want to be pretty for someone.
I want to be kissed softly.
I want to be someone's girlfriend
So, so bad.

I was good at being the skin's lie.
I did hard things that only the lie could do.
I achieved much as only the privileged lie could.
I was still a girl, but the lie prevailed.

Now, I am lost.
So many say they understand,
But no one wants to hold my hand.
No one wants to experience the beautiful girl that is me.

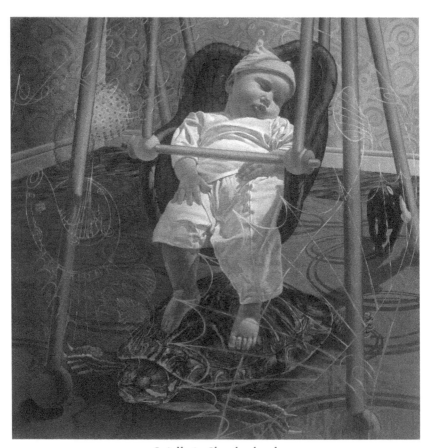

Arielle in Slumberland

I Am on the Path

I am on the path,
The path I yearned for since childhood.
The first step took me most of my life.
The path leading to this path:
One of secrecy.

The path I am on now,
The one of my dreams,
It's still so long.
It's still very hard.
I am not even close to done.

Oh ... so far to go.
Already happier than I have ever been.
Becoming a girl—
Such a beautiful thing
Only girls like me understand.

I am a girl now.
I have achieved that goal.
Right now, I am the only one who truly knows
I am a girl all the way in my heart.
Why do I reach yet further?

I reach always for more:
More of the complete dream,
The dream I had as a little girl
Locked in the lie of a little boy.
I now reach past "I am a girl now."

The dream was of a boy I knew.
The dream was to be his girlfriend.
The dream was to be loved—
Loved as only a girl can be.
The dream was to be a real girl.

I reach to fulfill that little girl's dream.
That little girl's boys are gone.
I have done almost everything I can do.
I have come so far, but still, I wait.
I want a man to say he loves me too.

Finally Want a Man

I finally want a man.
I really want one to be with,
I want to be a girl with,
To be a woman with.
I spent my life wanting to be a girl,
A girl who had a boyfriend,
A boyfriend that saw me as his girl.
No one but I could see the girl in me.
I finally want a man.
I never crossed that line before.
It always had to be
A man with his girlfriend ... Me?
No one could see me.
I was the only one,
The only one to quietly believe
Someday someone would see
I finally want a man.
I always wanted a man.
I finally want a man,
Out loud.
I always could see the girl in me.
I didn't always hide her so well.
Hidden away, she was;
The exterior boy a shell.
Three months ago,
My breasts were one year old.
In three weeks,
My vagina will turn one.
Estrogen will have ruled
Three years next November.
A woman's libido
Rises to my surface skin.
I finally want a man.

I finally gave myself permission.
I finally said that I am not the only one to see—
To see the beautiful girl that has been hiding inside of me.
I finally want a man.
I want a man
Who finally wants me.

The Trauma of It All

The trauma of it all,
The absolute joy,
The limitations of reality,
The clash of the three.

To hide a life
Not always so well hidden,
To deny a self
That will never go away.

To undo the sketchy,
The public figure on display,
Always failing to meet
The expectations of the feigned.

The trauma of it all:
Torn, a lifelong tear,
Silently
Dodging being torn apart.

Ripping off a piece,
Putting it away in a secret place,
It grows back slightly wiser,
Like a lizard's tail.

How to be
That which never was:
At some point, keep the tail.
Throw the rest away.

The absolute joy—
Finally—
No longer someone
A feigned façade.

Now, to be someone
True,
Hidden so long,
Someone still unknown.

The absolute joy
Watching a new and beautiful tail grow—
The tale of a life
No longer in a secret place.

Pleasures so private.
Others wiggle when shared.
Parthenogenesis
In self-loves purest form.

Trauma didn't abate.
The feigned life's demise
A life's vacuum to be filled;
Trauma will always have a place.

The absolute joy
Shouldering trauma;
Trauma chosen,
Not imposed.

The absolute joy.
Pain—
Only with decision's pain
Is the new tail real.

The absolute joy,
All the little special things,
Hidden secrets only surmised in fantasy
Embracing the tail become real.

A tale of a tail, torn off and hidden.
Allowed; Ontogeny set free.
How close to Phylogeny
Will the tail's tale be?

Oh ... the absolute joy.
More than a just a joy—
A soft, quiet smile.
Contentment to be.

The limitations of reality:
What has been done
To what could be
But could be no more?

Reality confines a path.
Easy ... Follow the signs of stampede,
Still fear in living up to the steps
Taken by so many.

The limitations of reality:
To break free of serendipity,
Changes that cannot be.
Serendipity prayer is a lie.

There is no path not walked before.
Serendipity an excuse.
Accept the joy of the easy path.
Don't challenge courage's muster.

The wisdom to know
Cowardice, often the fateful guide.
Cowardice vs courage,
Every wisdom unique.

There is no path not walked before.
The faintness of earlier footfall,
Courage, almost uniquely wise;
Steps taken others can see.

The limitations of reality—
Herd health: Don't stray;
Stray with controlled fear;
Define courage, define oneself

The trauma of it all,
A life unlived, hidden,
A self finally exposed and free,
A new herd to be found.

The trauma of it all,
The absolute joy,
The limitations of reality—
Absolute joy steps to the fore.

The clash challenges,
The wisdom of courage,
A life unlived, hidden,
Dies by one's own hand.

Wise courage is not courage;
Wise courage is safe.
Die in place by one's own hand,
Or let the unlived life out.

There Is No Such Thing as a Foolish Dream

I am on the path of a foolish dream,
Trying to be something I was only in my dreams,
And yet never was.
The conflict now is beyond the evident,
And because of the evident,
I told a shop owner
I was a transgender girl.
Guess what she said: "No, you're not."
For you ... Woman is all that is left.
Just because I am an old man that wants to become a girl,
She saw the "old he" on the other side of my "young she."
She pronounced that being a girl was long gone;
Settle for old lady.
What was in her words disturbed my dream.
I remember reevaluating my dreams.
I almost decided she was right.
I have gone this far ... Yeah, settle for sitting in a rocking chair.
So, there I was.
I spent several months investigating the logic of what she said.
Don't you hate it when someone is right?
Several months' work giving up a dream;
I slowly returned to not caring anymore.

The Fairer hand

Finish Becoming a Girl

I will finish becoming a girl
In the next three months.
I read the above two lines and think, *How absurd.*
Yes, my breasts will be big; I think they say "augmented."
I already have puffed-up lips.
My eyebrow skull has been shaved.
My jaw bone has been shaved too.
My nose is distinctly smaller, with a little bit of a ski jumpers' slope.
Crazy!
Yes, I think I am crazy too.
In two weeks, I have the finishing facial feminization lift.
In two months after that, vaginoplasty.
This is not much of a poem,
I am just trying to set the stage for you.
I will only be as close as I can be
Physically.
Mentally is a completely different thing.
I am getting there.
I have a psychologist
Walking along with me as I navigate this path.
I read Jennifer's books;
She frequently returns to question:
How far away is her "he" from her now?
I have the same discussion with myself.
I know that my "him" always had a "her" inside.
My "her" gave me so much more guidance than my "he" ever could.
So, no,
I didn't classically have a "she" past,
But I had a "she" that was hid, but very clear to me.
So many friends liked me, maybe slightly more privately
Because I was a softer version of a "he."
So, now I try to step away from hiding my "she"
Physically and mentally.
On both, while I won't fail, I also won't truly prevail.
There is no finish line;
I will never see the pot at the end of the rainbow until I die.

At least, I hope I see it then.

It's never been about the pot;

It's always been about the rainbow.

Physically becoming a girl, at least as close as I can get,

Is a tool to support me mentally.

I know "cis" is out of reach.

Contentment is right there on the edge of my own mind.

I am past trying to convince you;

I am working on convincing me.

I already—as in now—walk down the street as a girl.

That was the goal.

From the first day I tried to act as a girl some sixty years ago

Until now, and until I die,

I will always ask myself,

Did I do that right?

All the do's, all the do's ...

I will never have "cis" confidence.

That is where my psychologist comes into play.

I have to mentally know

That "cis", which means "real",

Is out of reach for many "cis" girls too.

Everyone struggles with "real."

What the hell is "real", and who defines "real" too?

I think I am almost there.

I have revisited my visions of being a "girl"—

Secret visions from sixty-five years.

I think I saw a hope and a goal,

Just like any little "cis" girls do.

To grow up to be like my big sister, or my mom,

To grow up to be like the popular girls in school,

Hell, even to grow up to be a nun instead of a priest.

So, the "cis" girl's path to be the next step in "girl"

Was maybe slightly easier than the same path for me.

It doesn't matter.

That is what the psychologist taught me.

I never strayed.

Every step I made

Always took into consideration

The girl in me.

That's all the "cis" girls could do;

That's all I could do too.
You know, it's not a race.
Many "cis" girls believed in themselves as girls
Long before I did.
Many "cis" girls did not.
Please notice past tense—
Thank you, psychologist,
And thank me too.
I never strayed.
That's what made the difference:
The continuous thread of the girl I am.
From the first day,
I am a girl;
I am only going to get better.

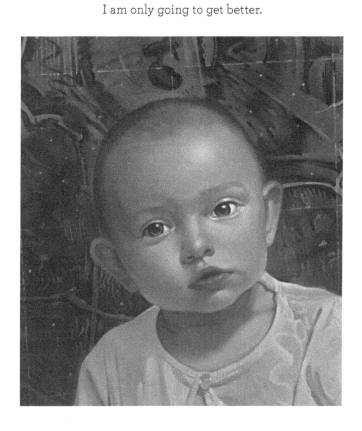

I Will Never be Alone as Long as There is You

Today, I spent an hour with you.
How am I, how am I doing too?
Only you know what I am going through.
You know almost better than I do.
It is so hard to see tomorrow.
It is so hard to see my way through,
But you are there with me.
Tomorrow is no more clear to you,
But you step forward too.
I finally know I am not alone.
I will make my mistakes
With you
Watching lovingly over me.
Today, I felt so bad
About how I said how I feel.
I think you know.
I need say nothing more
Except:
"I will never be alone as long as there is you."

Getting ready

How Bad Do You Want to be a Girl?

How bad do you want to be a girl?
How bad do you want to be a girl?
How bad do you want to be a girl?
How bad do you want to be a girl?
How bad do you want to be a girl?
How bad do you want to be a girl?
How bad do you want to be a girl?
Really?
How bad?
I am a girl now.
Okay ... not really,
But as close as I can get ... be.
This question, answered,
Means nothing.
A thousand times posed,
Silently answered.
How bad do you want to be a girl?
Such a stupid question.
Such a stupid question.
Such a stupid question.
Because you are not.
I never asked myself this question even once.
Why am I not a girl?
Why can't I be a girl?
Do I have to live as not a girl?
I wish I was a girl.
If I was a girl I would ...
Even these are too direct.
Years of hiding myself
From everyone but me.
A small flower would bud ... maybe bloom ...
Silently pray,
Can I be your girl?
Can I be me to you?

Please let me be a girl.
These are the questions you needed to have asked.
How bad do you want to be a girl?
Means
You don't want to be a girl bad enough,
At least not yet.
I do not understand any of this.
I can give no solace.
You have to cry a thousand tears
A thousand times.
You have to walk away from a life you yearned
But could not have.
You have to resign yourself to the life you have …
Yet it never is enough.
You silently see every event through the eyes of someone:
Hidden,
Little happinesses.
You spin in your heart with a girlish joy.

BE BOLD AND MIGHTY FORCES WILL COME TO YOUR AID

Tom Over Manana

Hi

Hi.
Yes, Hi.
I am still here.
I lose track of what I am going to type.
I want to say thank you to everyone
Before I say goodbye.
A path that alienates everyone,
Everyone but me.
I have friends that killed themselves.
Are they better off?
Are they better off than me?
Do I need to be happy for one bright moment
Then say goodbye?
Would I care?
Would you care?
Would anyone care?
At what point do I kill myself?
Not today.
Tomorrow is inconvenient too.
Not too far away,
I need to stop.
I need to stop.
What the hell does "stop" mean?
I am never going to hurt myself;
That doesn't mean I don't want to.
Come and get me, life.
Come and take me out, so that I don't have to.
I am tired now.
I am so tired.
I have to believe in me.

I have to believe in the girl I am going to be.
I am such a joke to everyone.
I write each line only after the last line is written.
It will never end now.
Yes, I will move.

Note: Gender dysphoria and the process of transgender transition have both been linked to depression. Psychological support is critical to a healthy outcome.

53rd High School Reunion

Return

Return.
Return to what?
Return to a place or time
That no longer exists.

Return to a memory;
Old memories
Of pain forgotten,
Where happy thoughts remain.

Return.
Return as the conquering hero,
The success that occurred so long ago,
To reclaim the dreams of a life you earlier left.

To step back into who you were.
A part of a society that you can enter
To forget the reason you left.
Did it ever include return?

There is no such thing as "return."
There is no *there*, there anymore.
You are not who you were.
Where you return to is not what you left.

You do not have to go anywhere
To not be able to return,
Not even to yesterday.
You don't belong in or to yesterday anymore.

To attempt to "belong",
To return to a "belonging",
You have to give away a piece of you.
What you then belong to will hesitate to give you back.

Do you know what it means
To give away a piece of your soul,
To laugh at the right jokes,
To wear the right collared shirt?

To "belong" is to acquiesce
To consensus:
To date the right girl, to drink the right drink,
Return to belong to not yourself.

You can't return.
There is no such thing.
The best you can do
Is arrive anew.

Do you need to leave?
Have you lost yourself and are adrift?
Do you not see your tomorrows holding dreams
Yet fulfilled?

Leave if you must.
You have barely scratched your opportunities here,
The people that love you here,
The tomorrows you are yet to dream.

Leave if you must;
Leave if you just want to,
But don't call it "returning."
It's leaving.

This poem's true title is "Leaving."

Homeless

Homeless ... I have been homeless.
I have been homeless at home;
I have been homeless without a home.
Homelessness is reflectively sad, and oddly powerful.
Homelessness is the unwritten sign:
"You don't belong here ... Keep moving."
As a child, you walk past your siblings', "Hey ... scram!"
As an adult. you walk down roads without a destination.
Homelessness is wearing out your welcome,
Hearing voices: "Quiet ... Shhh!"
Homelessness is walking on until tired.
Homelessness is finding a kind field before sunset.
There is so much power in homelessness.
One must realize the gift "homeless" carries:
No longer living up to another's expectations,
Finally realizing you need to have your own.
A goal that can't be reached ... by the homeless.
Respect that can't be earned ... by the homeless.
A meal that can't be eaten ... by the homeless.
Clothes that can't be washed ... by the homeless.
Homeless is a type of bottom
Where many go to drug and drink.
Drug and drink often showed the way,
Redefined the bottom every day.
For the few that are only homeless,
A special power avails itself.
The freedom to prove yourself to yourself again:
You're homeless ... no one else cares.
A job where you don't really know how to tell them where you live:
Clothes washed in sinks, food in dumpsters,
Sleeping in the basement laundry room of a hospital,
Hiding in the stack spaces of a library.
Work your way back up until you can afford a second shirt,
Get a job in a restaurant washing the dishes,
Outworking everyone that washed dishes before you.
Get a minimal raise, a taste of respect,

Walk into a junior college barefoot,
Wearing Arthur Ash shorts and your second shirt.
Ask without pride,
"Can I go to college here?"
Leave behind the open road,
The things thrown at you from trucks.
Leave behind the beauty of spiders
Weaving crystalline nets as the sun sets.
Leave behind singing Janis Joplin songs:
"Freedom is just another word
For nothing left to lose
And
Nothing ain't nothing if it ain't free."
Leave behind "skin popping turpentine"
And dropping masculine.
Leave behind the rare joint and the rare friend.
Laughter around a fire in the woods.
Would you rather sit outside an RV,
Watching a large, flat-screen TV?
The power of homelessness:
If you own yourself, you are always home.
A homeless Vietnam veteran
In college receives the G.I. Bill,
A small, shared apartment and spartan meals,
A second pair of pants, a third shirt … and shoes.
Between twenty-two and thirty-five,
Homeless in the full definition of the word.
At least five years of worn welcomes,
But so many beautiful evenings of spider art.
Most in life count a person's worth in the work they do;
That's really all a truly homeless person has to give.
Honesty, Reliability, Consistency:
The three pillars of a progressive soul.
The homeless, the truly homeless,
Have to learn to give something more.
They have to learn to give themselves
Love.
Only with love can a spirit survive.
The homeless must learn to love themselves—
Love that stands on the three-legged stool of

Honesty, Reliability, Consistency.
If you wonder what it would be like to be homeless,
You never were.
Stop wondering.
It's hard enough without wanting to know.

Favorite Wig

The Psychology of Me

Here I am,
Almost done.
A girl is only months away.
I look back on all I have said and done,
Hoping that some people might understand.
They can't.
I so know that now.
Lost.
So many people lost to me,
Because I want to be a girl.
Within every poem I say this:
I have always wanted to be a girl,
And
I really did.
Time … Time went by.
Almost a whole lifetime passed.
Now I know,
I also came to not want to be me.
Facial feminization, one and two.
Breast augmentation.
I finally don't see him.
How much of me was "don't be him"?
How much of me was "be a girl"?
The balance I don't know.
The more I move forward on this path,
The more I know how broken I was.
I also know
That I will never be okay,
Not really.
I moved away from a comfortable life
That was slowly killing me.
I saw my death.
I had to decide;
Make a change or die.
I never wanted to be a man,
But a man I was.

Back in 1974, I almost stayed in Hawaii
To become a male prostitute,
Wearing a badge saying,
"I am a boy."
I wanted more than that future held
How many gay bars did I go to
Dressed in drag?
"You're not good at this," I was told.
"Shave your mustache and try again."
Transgenderism is its own weird cork
I want to experience a man,
Yet I am not gay.
I mostly just want to be a girl.
I can't really see me as a woman,
An old girl with tits,
But that is exactly where I am.
My mind,
The psychology of me,
I finally am not him.
I don't see him anymore.
Why is that so important to me?
Why do I want too never be him again?
What part of me grew to hate being him?
I led him, but did he own me.
Break, break away.
Leave him behind, think of him no more.
I don't want to remember his past.
I don't want credit for all the good or bad he did.
One hundred thousand dollars of facial surgery.
I was told repeatedly,
"You don't have to do that to be a girl,"
But I did.
I see that clearly now.
To become a girl, I had to kill him first.
So, months and months of pain
Just to set me free.
It's all psychology.
I was broken, in pain, and so unhappy.
I couldn't continue anymore,
Being a man I never wanted to be.

Every male friend has left me now,
And most female friends too.
I am a very young, seventy-year-old girl,
Just now going through puberty.
Soon I will be a virgin all over again.
Damn the psychology.
I am going to move away,
Leave Maine behind me too.
Start new, start me, start again.
So much I have to do to psychologically handle being the new me.
My psychologist has helped me more than I can ever express.
I was going somewhere before I ever talked to her.
Where I was going was not healthy.
I am a girl now,
A virgin.
Never been on a serious date.
At seventy, how do I be sixteen?
That's the girl my psychology wants me to be.
I have to grow past that now.
I have to learn how to be an old lady.
I will take it.
That is
the psychology of me.

It's Hard to Write a
Poem Right Now

A poem is on the edge of my lips,
My swollen lips that are very sore.
I can't seem to get past the sore aspect of my lips.
I had my lips augmented
The upper, of course, but the lower too.
Now, I don't have one sore lip, I have two.
My nose also is very sore.
Oh, the rhinoplasty; plasty is a tough word to a nose.
Someday, hopefully soon, I will see my new nose.
Right now, it is under a cast.
I sleep on and off,
I wait for healing to round the bend.
I am swollen now, and I don't look like a girl.
My lips hopefully will calm down.
My nose will come out from under the cast.
It is so crazy to want results as these.
I want my nose to say "girl."
I want my lips to say "you can kiss me."
I may never get there in your mind;
That's OK.
My mind's having a hard time too.
I am still going to go there
With or without you.

Thanksgiving Dinner 2023

Hi, Again

"Hi," is what I will say,
Sitting on a bar stool.
So many people that know me just feet away.
All of this will be in a year past.
I will wait for a man that sees only me,
A girl,
Sitting on a bar stool.
I will go home after one beer,
Like a thousand times before.
I will look in the mirror and ask,
Did I do the right thing?
I already know that I am, and eventually, did.
This is the right thing for me.
I may only find joy in being pretty,
Shaving my legs and wearing a dress,
Being soft as the girl I fantasize.
I will go downtown again and again,
Visit everyone that knew "him."
They will have to decide:
Became a "girl" ... is "he" still inside?
You know, I don't care.
The girl I am was always there.
I am going to lead a progressive life.
I will give no-quarter to anyone.
Few real girls will want to spend time with me,
As an interloper who can't possibly understand.
Men will also avoid me.
"Am I queer to be with her; she once was a man."
I didn't do all of this to be with them;
I did it all to be with me.
So, now I sit and write this poem.
It's 1:00 a.m., my sister in the next bed asleep.
She is here taking care of me.
She is worried about me physically and mentally.
I understand this.
I will have to understand this so much more.

The challenge is just beginning.
So, I write this poem to remind myself.
To remind myself
My tomorrows are going to be long.
Long, and most likely alone.
I need to be what I have always been
My only champion.
I already see my life before me
I actually watch me push people away
What was offered was pity.
No, no.
I only want to know that if I had been a girl
All this time,
Would I have been happy?
Girl ... pink ... princess
fantasy.
Remember, Reader: I am sixty-nine.

Butterfly Tattoo
In honor of the Papillon Center in New Hope, PA
where I received my ultimate feminizing surgery

Looking Back

Looking back ... but why?
Looking back to see some form of consistency.
Looking back to justify my now and my tomorrow.
Looking back to feel the pain,
To know your happier now.

Dancing with my sisters in their room,
Wearing a little dress,
Twirling like a little girl,
Knowing I belonged at age four.
That was the goal that day.

Kissing a boy,
Convincing him we needed to practice,
Learning how to hug and hold a boy.
I was seven, and daddy caught me.
Kissing: that was the goal that day.

Mommy's boy.
By mom's side, this little girl would stay.
How many times did daddy say,
"You are not a girl!"
But that was the goal that day.

Going to the park at age eight,
Sitting with the girls
Where I belonged, where I wanted to stay,
Making pot-holders as the boys came to hit me.
Pot-holders: that was the goal that day.

My friends were girls;
The boys I feared.
The girls grew up becoming little women;
They all slowly moved away from me.
I wanted to be a girl so bad; that was the goal that day.

Silently living alone at age thirteen,
Buying Kotex and wearing them in my pants
Every month for several days,
To be a girl, to be a girl just a little bit.
To somehow fit: that was the goal that day.

Living lost and alone,
Not belonging to a clan of boys or girls,
Watching boys and men do such stupid things.
A boy or a man I never wanted to be.
To hide the girl inside: that was the goal that day.

Met a boy overseas, a coast guardsman I was.
Charlie; I will never not remember him.
One day, I told him I loved him and gave him a gentle hug.
He stepped back and stared at me, never to speak to me again.
To tell a man I loved him: that was the goal that day.

At age twenty-three, another man—Oh! Again, I fell in love—
We biked together; we shared life without a single touch.
I didn't say "I love you"; I hid my girl away.
I think he loved me, too, but I will never know.
Don't scare him away: that was the goal that day.

Throughout the years, only my special friends knew.
Birthdays and Christmas: buy me a dress, maybe panties too.
At twenty-five, I wore panties under my pants,
A girl sitting up straight that you can't see right in front of you.
To be a girl and hide her too: that was the goal that day.

Belly-dancing became a secret I could no longer hide.
A full year training as a belly-dancing girl,
So happy as I swirled and twisted as only a girl could do,
Informed I had to start being a male belly-dancer …
I put the girl back away: that was the goal that day.

Looking back at so much pain,
I hate it as I write this poem.
I cry at all the things I could have been
But never was allowed.

A girl hidden away: that was the goal that day.

Senior year at a very small college
I attended as a girl,
There was so much happiness to be had—
Short skirts and panties, and a blouse on a flat chest.
I was almost a girl: that was the goal that day.

I came home once, forgetting to take off my dress.
I walked in the house to my father's stare.
He approached me with an anger I knew too well.
A brutal clutch, through clenched teeth, "I will kill you if you're a fag."
I ran away: that was the goal that day

Thirty-four years in the military.
For thirty-four years, I hid me the girl.
When you don't belong anywhere,
The military is a great place to hide your secrets away.
They didn't ask, and I didn't tell: that was the goal that day.

Married to have a family.
At least I could be a sweet dad.
Years later I retired; no kids, no grandchildren,
A life of hiding the true me drove me to drink.
Drunk: that was the goal that day.

I was on the verge of suicide.
I had a twelve gauge; I planned the way.
I didn't want to die, I wanted to be a girl.
I finally chose to be a girl over all else.
Divorced, but a girl: that was the plan that day.

Two visits to the emergency room,
Two stays in a detox center,
Three months in alcohol recovery camp.
I am a girl, and I am sober.
I am a sober girl: that was the plan that day.

So, I look back and see all the things wanting to be a girl has done to me.
I never stopped, not one day.

I don't understand it any more than you;
I only know that my wanting to be a girl is true.
I am a girl now: that was the goal that day, and from now on.

I look back and revisit myself.
I need to, so I don't forget what I have been through.
A man in a restaurant at another table called me a faggot three times.
One of a thousand slights that hurt, yet not at all.
I am a girl; I am a girl … finally.

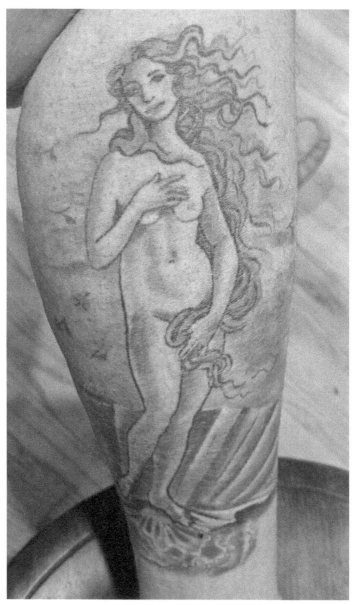

The Birth of Lukcia
A tattoo modeled after Sandro Botticelli's painting
The Birth of Venus

Looking Forward

I am looking forward now,
Past becoming a girl.
I look forward to refining her,
To make her happy to be,
Because she is me.

I look forward to every pretty dress.
I buy them, and they usually look crazy on me.
I am six foot tall and weigh two hundred ten.
I have so many dresses that I wear only at home.
They were cut for a different-sized girl.

I study cosmetics at Ulta and online.
I look forward to making up my face.
I have had all the surgeries,
So now my panties fit ... they fit ... they fit ... they fit!
I look down and see a girl between my legs ... mmm ... so happy!

My breasts I grew while on hormones,
They seem to be growing still.
I love them.
I look forward to walking with them out in front.
They're my girls, and they're right where they should be.

I met a boy and dated a few times.
His male and female friends told him to back away.
I am a "New Cougar" now.
I am on the prowl;
Only a special man will do.

I can't believe how much I love to dream.
In my dreams, I am now always a girl.
While I have never been with a man,
In my dreams I go where I have never been before.
I look forward to when that man is real.

I am learning how to be a girl
As only a girl can be.
I have a few girlfriends now.
We get together and have fun,
As only girls can do.

I have my whole body hot-waxed every six weeks,
Smooth skin that I absolutely love.
I love how a delicate dress feels against my legs:
Lovely, smooth, soft.
Some man will get to feel.

I look forward to a boyfriend;
It could happen, but it may not.
I can't let that sadden me.
I have so much to look forward to.
Then I will get old and die a girl.

Hormone Replacement Therapy
A beautiful truth of Male-to-Female Transition
I love being estrogen based

I Don't Make Men Tingle

I don't make men tingle.
I learned this in a hard way.
I wish I stayed unaware
That men don't tingle because I am there.

I met a man so fine and smart.
He was six foot four,
Taller than me by just the right amount.
He knew me for who I am, but I guess only being kind.

Two dates in,
Two dinners that were very fine,
Hoping for a handhold or a kiss—
A "sorry for you" hug, and gone.

Two days later, I got the text:
"We can only be friends.
I hope that is OK."
I tried to delete him from my heart as I cried myself to sleep.

"We can only be friends"
Usually means
"I plan to never see you again;
I'm just being polite."

Weeks later, I started to receive his texts.
Maybe only friends;
One never knows what friends can do.
Maybe there is cautious hope.

This man of my dreams continued to communicate.
It was nice.
Friendship was better than nothing.
Organically, I would wait.

This man continued to share his life,
Little stories that were happening to him
At a lawn party while on vacation,
The guest of honor in his hometown.

This man told me of a discovery:
A woman some forty-odd feet away.
He could see her;
He wondered who she was.

She noticed him, too,
Walked his way,
Touched him genteelly on his arm.
His response gave him alarm.

So, he told me in his text:
"When she touched me,
My whole body tingled,
Like lightning struck; my hair stood up."

This man, my only-a-friend,
Just crushed my heart.
I will get over him.
I am over him now.

I went to bed.
I cried that night.
I don't make men tingle;
What's to become of me?

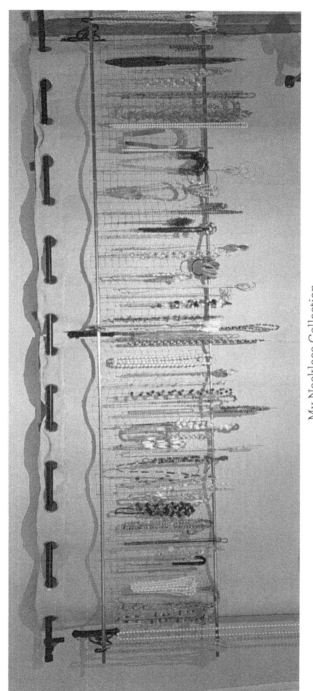

My Necklace Collection

I Stand Alone

I stand alone,
Looking out into the epidemy of darkness,
Looking deeply into the darkness,
And up into the twinkling sky.

I stand alone.
I should be celebrating, but I am not.
It's December the twenty-first,
The Winter Solstice.

What to do about him …
His days grew shorter until that day,
His birthday since 1952.
He is no longer here.

I stand alone.
I am no longer him.
I no longer celebrate his special day.
I no longer feel any loyalty at all.

For so long, I honored him
For hiding me so well,
For getting me here safely, on this day.
So, I can finally say farewell.

I owe him much, and yet owe him nothing at all.
He would want it that way.
He had honor, and when he gave a gift,
The gift was truly given, no strings attached.

I stand alone
On his special day
And say goodbye one last time;
Only the gift remains … the gift of me.

I lay on a gurney,
Hooked up to tubes and needles.
Alone I lay, waiting;
I am soon to sleep.

Awake and aware that I am stepping away from him,
The doctor steps close.
"Are you ready?" Yes ... I have never not been.
"Okay, let's give you a beautiful girl."

I wake up.
As soon as I could muster words,
"Give me a mirror, please.
I need to see her; I need to see her now."

There she was.
He was gone.
I cried.
I cried the cry of a lifetime lost.

I speak of this moment,
And I still cry today.
I finally met the me I knew was always there.
The Tenth of May 2022:
My birthday.
I knew that I was born that day.
The past of him faded away.

Girlfriends that became a girl as I did,
They understand.
Each of us knows our birthday,
No longer to celebrate his again.

I stand alone,
Looking into the epidemy of dark.
I was born only seven months ago.
I celebrate not celebrating him.

I don't consider him dead,
Nor is his name my dead name;
He is just not here anymore.
His job was done; he went away.

"Oh!" my girlfriends ask,
"How are you going to celebrate your birthday?"
I don't know; I really don't.
It's so exciting to think; soon I will be *one!*

They push me for plans, but I still don't know.
Tongue-in-cheek, I tell them,
"I am going to put one candle in her, light it,
And find someone to blow it out."

It is so fun to think about the girl I am and am going to become.
My first birthday came and went.
In eleven months, I will be *two.*
What will a two-year-old girl at age seventy do?

Why ... progressively put more candles in her,
Light them,
And pray ...
A man blows them out.

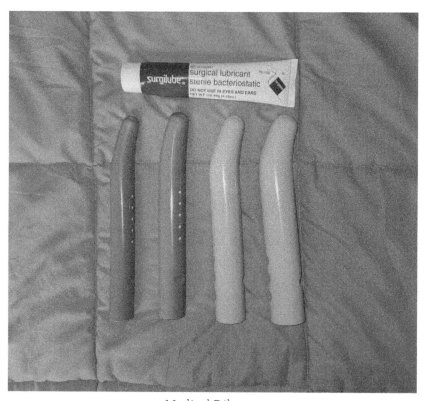

Medical Dilators
A truth associated with Male-to-female Transition
Maintaining the young lady

Sexuality

Oh, what to do now that I am her?
How far away from "him" can "she" me be?
A challenge for her to define her sexuality:
Does his past control where she can go?

Is his past that which everyone saw,
Or is his past what she quietly knew?
Transition is breaking expectations imposed.
What lies in a new girl's heart; does the new girl know?

The courage to continue a path of discovery,
The challenge to find yet more that's true;
Every day know a little more of myself.
Questions must be asked to guide the way.

New expectations imposed on a new girl.
It's okay to date someone just like yourself.
It's okay if you are also gay.
That's what they already think of me.

Do they pressure me because I became a girl
Or is it because I gave up being a man?
What kind of misogyny will now be imposed?
Don't you dare try to love a real man.

A real man, cis man, cis woman, me;
Freedom to choose like any cis person eludes.
Did I break free into a larger cage,
A maze of paths allowed, or break yet more walls down?

With time, I have come to know my true self.
I want to be with a cis man,
A cis man who loves me.
Am I inviting him to be my lover, or just into my cage?

If a cis man falls in love with me,
He will no longer be a cis man philosophically.
He will be somewhere between heterosexual and queer—
The no man's land of dating a female facsimile.

Cis men can have the courage to decide,
Courage similar to that which allowed me to be a she.
Love without courage is ultimately
Controlled by family, friends, and fear.

I only speak for me as a transgender woman.
I don't speak for anyone else.
Every woman is unique.
That also applies to me.

I love a man: I see him as the beautiful man he is;
I believe he can see the woman that is me.
What part of his life will be taken away
If he gives me the same gift I offer him?

The courage of a transgender woman is almost beyond compare.
How can one expect a mare-man to such a courage bear?
I walked away from almost every aspect of my life to become a she;
To ask that of another is too much—that courage is too rare.

I am a girl now.
If that is all I ever get,
I got enough.
I am happy, and I don't ideate hurting myself anymore.

It is healthy to want more;
To not want more is to die a slow, spiritual death.
I hope to grow old, to eventually die,
But I will never stop wanting a man.

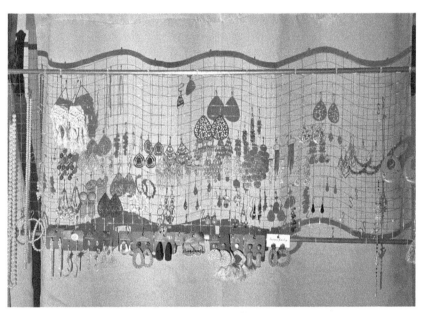

My Earring Collect

The Last Talk to Myself

I am Lukcia now.
"No turning back" happened long ago.
Now I feel complete:
A girl, attempted love, tomorrows becoming today.

Challenges don't stop.
Hell! I don't even know what will happen to my body
When I finally die as the girl I so recently became:
A solemn goodbye, or will politics interfere?

Attempted love as a woman three times now;
All ultimately played out the same.
Each time, when I knew the end had already passed,
I thanked them for allowing me to learn.

I still occasionally see one of them
In their professional capacity,
One is emails and texts,
The last is truly gone.

Of the three, only one actually asked me out.
The other two, I asked out.
All three are physically gone to me now;
Only the one is emails and texts.

I can't see the email man again.
I already laid my cards down.
He folded; he didn't want to play.
He is now anywhere other than here with me.

The three wise men that came to visit me,
As in a manger, I was newly born;
They gave me three different gifts of wisdom,
Wisdom needed to carry on.

I can't ask any of them out again;
That option now only theirs.
They know that; they know what that means.
Together; they have to want that too.

I fell in love with two of these men
For significantly different reasons,
Of which being selfish was one.
I need to love organically and stop selfish pursuit.

I can't see these two men casually.
Never again will my heart not weep.
To be with either and know ...
I will start to cry; I will have to run away.

I was—am—a brand-new girl,
Prayed for a quick resolve.
A man shows up and loves me now,
So I could finish my life in bliss.

If they called me up and asked me out—
Yes, to one, to the other two no—
I hope it happens, but doubt it will.
He knows what that ask implies.
Why did I think someone my age would understand?
Two people can create romance and love;
A first touch tingle does not need prevail.
There is so much more to a girl; first you must lift the veil.

I will take the wisdoms given me.
Maybe future opportunities will come to me.
I will try to do things organically.
I will try, but my love is on my sleeve.

A sad part of me knows that the future yet untold,
May find me looking back,
Seeing love's opportunities untaken:
Two now really old people left to die alone.

This is my last talk to myself.
These talks are a tool to keep me strong.
I am Lukcia now; I am a girl.
I have to get on with life.

Divorce Settlement Celebration Dinner
My Ex-wife and I are still very good friends

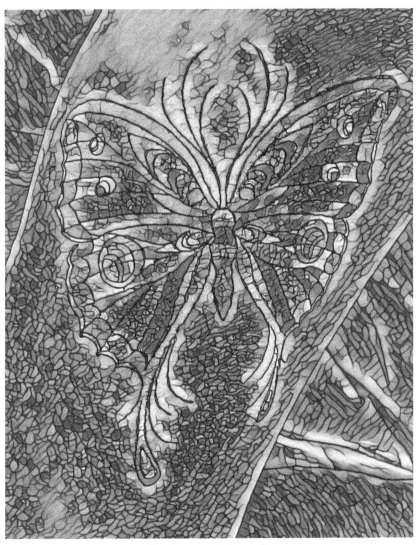

The Fractured Butterfly
I have emerged from my chrysalis
Now I need plenty of space to stretch my wings and learn to fly

The Reason for the Bangor Daily News Article

I knew my whole life that I wanted to be a girl, and at no time did this want abate. I was realistic and pursued a life as a male because I had no other choice. At the age sixty-seven, I finally felt free of the obligations that were acquired during a long and progressive life. Retired and soon-to-be divorced, no children, and financially secure, I made the decision to do what was out-of-reach for so many years.

I know what difficulties I had, because a hidden truth shadowed every action, every career move, every relationship. I suffered as I went through life not fitting in with most any otherwise socially acceptable group. My marriage suffered. As a child I was molested, and as a young adult I was raped. Predators could see the person I was not allowed to be and took advantage of me. I felt very alone for the majority of my life.

I contacted the Bangor Daily News and offered to allow them to follow me through my transition to a female. They agreed, and the article to follow is the result.

If this article helps anyone to better understand themselves, to being open to accepting themselves, or if it helps people that don't understand gender dysphoria to have more compassionate thoughts about those that do, then the goal of the article was met.

Gender dysphoria is real and profoundly affects those who suffer from it. Treatment starts with compassion, understanding, and acceptance. My journey was fairly comprehensive, but also very expensive. Everyone's gender dysphoria is different, and everyone must find their own way, but all need compassion and acceptance.

Lukcia Patricia Sullivan was assigned male at birth and presented as a man for the first 67 years of her life. The Bangor Daily News followed Sullivan, 69, for the past year as she underwent a series of surgeries to align her body with her gender identity. Credit: Linda Coan O'Kresik / BDN

Suppressed for 67 years, a transgender woman finds her voice

by **Lia Russell**

241

August 1, 2022   Updated August 8, 2022

Lukcia Sullivan ran her hand across her scalp as Dr. Jeffrey Spiegel checked the IV line in her other arm and asked her about any allergies. It was a routine morning for the surgeon. But it was momentous for Lukcia, 69, who had been waiting for this day for decades, ever since she knew she was a girl.

In a few moments, she would be wheeled into the operating room of a clinic in Newton, Massachusetts. There, Spiegel and his team would spend the next six hours resculpting Lukcia's skull and facial tissues so she would appear more feminine. The procedure would involve narrowing her jaw, brow bone and chin; augmenting her lips; and reconstructing her nose.

Lukcia was assigned male at birth and presented as a man for the first 67 years of her life. Her sensitive nature made her a target of ridicule, however, first as a boy growing up in a rigidly traditional Irish-Catholic family, and later as a service member in the Coast Guard and U.S. Army. So she suppressed the mannerisms that others deemed too feminine and muted her true self to adapt to her gendered environs.

When she retired in 2018, she took stock of her life. She wanted to finally look like the woman she knew she was. Her surgery last December represented part of her transformation. Another step has involved reintroducing herself to her family and her community.

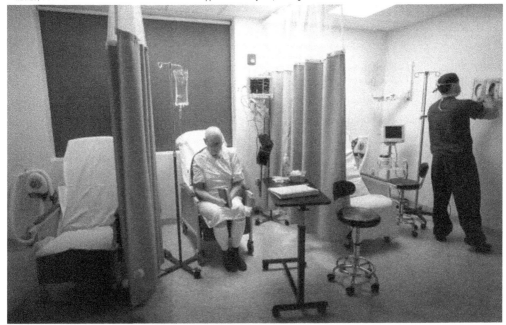

Lukcia Sullivan takes a moment to reflect before being taken into the operating room to undergo her first facial feminization surgery at the Spiegel Center in Newton, Massachusetts, on Dec. 14, 2021. Credit: Linda Coan O'Kresik / BDN

The Bangor Daily News followed Lukcia for a year as she underwent a series of surgeries to align her body with her gender identity after she began presenting as a woman in October 2020.

Lukcia wanted to show the world the realities and challenges of transitioning at an advanced age, even in a state like Maine that has some of the strongest available legal protections for LGBTQ residents. She wanted to send a message to younger people that they do not have to live their lives as someone they're not.

"There are other young men who don't need to live the lifestyle I did," she said.

What's more, sharing her story publicly would help her erase her previous life and any doubt people might have that Lukcia is a woman.

"I wanted to come out loud and proud," she said. "I didn't want people to whisper, 'Is there something going on with him?'"

For Lukcia, her journey is not complete without sharing it. It is important to her, regardless of what others think, that they at least know who she is. She has known for many years. Now comes the telling.

"The fact I subjected myself to so much intimate dialogue and detailed photography makes it real. [My identity] is not going to be able to be dismissed as easily, because it has depth and fabric," Lukcia said.

'Heading to see the wizard'

Pure grit and gratitude have shaped that fabric of her identity. Lukcia began hormone replacement therapy in November 2020, taking medication to help her body produce estrogen and suppress testosterone production. She grew breasts. Her skin softened. She cried more easily.

She officially changed her name last summer to Lukcia Patricia Sullivan, choosing a first name that honored Luke, the name she received at her first Holy Communion. She came home from the Bureau of Motor Vehicles after changing her name on her driver's license and cried for two hours.

Clockwise from top left: Lukcia Sullivan walks up her driveway to get the newspaper to read with her morning coffee on Dec. 8, 2021, days before her first of two facial feminization surgeries; Lukcia reads alone at the dining room table while drinking her morning coffee; Lukcia sits on the bathroom counter to be closer to the mirror while putting on makeup; Lukcia looks through the clothes hanging in her closet that reflect the girl she had known herself to be since the age of 4; Lukcia applies makeup most mornings, for which she is still learning techniques. Credit: Linda Coan O'Kresik / BDN

She adopted a uniform of elegant blouses, skirts and dresses, opting almost exclusively for soft pinks.

But it was while sitting in the surgical suite with Spiegel that it registered for Lukcia that her journey toward presenting as her true self had reached a critical point. She would undergo another facial feminization surgery with Spiegel two months later, then fly to Pennsylvania in May. There, she would receive a vaginoplasty from Dr. Christine McGinn, one of the world's top surgeons who specializes in transgender health care and who is also a transgender woman.

"I already knew I wasn't going back," Lukcia said. "That first surgery was the first step on the yellow brick road. I was heading to see the wizard."

That December morning, she forewent her usual silky blond wig. She arrived at the nondescript, monochrome clinic at 6 a.m. and donned a surgical gown. As she sat in a chair under harsh fluorescent lighting before the procedure began, she peppered Spiegel with questions about complications like swelling.

"Every woman has difficulty looking feminine," Spiegel reassured her. "They worry about aging, their facial structure, their skin quality. Don't worry. I've done this over a thousand times."

An assistant fitted a mask over her face, and she immediately dropped off to sleep. Spiegel and his team got to work.

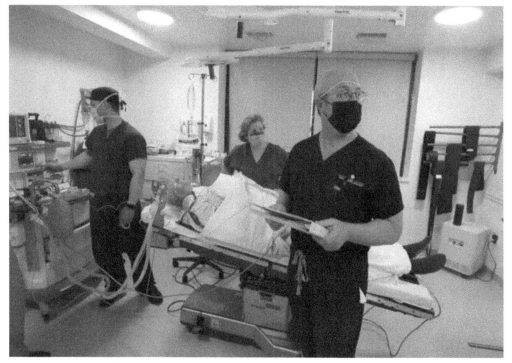

Dr. Jeffrey Spiegel of the Spiegel Center in Newton, Massachusetts, reads aloud the procedures that he will perform on Lukcia Sullivan for her first facial feminization surgery on Dec. 14, 2021. Credit: Linda Coan O'Kresik / BDN

'Girls did certain things, boys did certain things'

Lukcia's story began as the middle child of seven boys and girls in a family that not only rejected the idea that someone could be transgender but actively punished Lukcia for playing in ways her father thought was too feminine. She grew up in rural Harwinton, Connecticut, and gravitated toward female friends in her early adolescence. She was more interested in embroidery and cooking with her mother than anything her brothers did.

Her father tried vigorously to stamp that out and force her into more stereotypically male activities. He hit Lukcia every time he caught her dressing up in her sisters' clothes or playing house with other little girls. One of the last times they saw each other, in 1978, Lukcia's father threatened to kill her because he didn't want a "gay son," she said.

"In our family, things were very structured and regimented by sex," said Debbie Seymour, 68, Lukcia's sister. "Girls did certain things, the boys did certain things. My father really, truly believed that vacuuming would ruin a boy."

Transgender people have a different gender identity and expression than the one they were assigned at birth. Some transgender people, though not all, are diagnosed with gender dysphoria, a clinical set of criteria that refer to the persistent distress a person feels when their assigned sex doesn't match their gender identity.

Lukcia coped with that distress by tending to her family's farm animals, and she left her parents' home at 15 to live with other families while she attended an alternative high school for vocational agriculture. But she didn't escape the influence of her father, who forced her into the Coast Guard at 17 after a fight.

Her three years there led to more military service: She joined the Army to pay for college and graduate school in Florida to become a veterinarian. After graduating, she served in Bosnia, Germany and Iraq as an officer training dogs to sniff out bombs and landmines. She left active duty in 1994 and retired in 2004.

When she entered the military, she suppressed her feminine mannerisms and interests to adapt to the stringent, masculine environment, she said. She sometimes rented hotel rooms for a few hours so she could dress in the feminine clothing she longed to wear, away from judgmental bystanders.

It was the only place she could be herself, even if only momentarily.

In 1999, she moved to Maine to become a U.S. Department of Agriculture meat inspector. With her then-wife, she built a house on a plot of land in Hampden overlooking the Penobscot River. She designed it to reflect the principles of feng shui, the eastern art of placement, which she subscribed to as part of her Zen Buddhist beliefs.

Her vegetable garden beds lined each side of the house on steppes, as though they were the "wings of a dragon," she said.

When she retired in 2018, she reflected on her life. After coming out to her wife, the decline of her already unraveling marriage accelerated. It hadn't produced the children she wanted. Her former wife, whom she divorced earlier this month, declined to comment.

But those story endings meant a new one could begin. After nearly seven decades, it was time to become Lukcia.

Lukcia's reality

Lukcia Patricia Sullivan, 18, when she was undergoing boot camp in the U.S. Coast Guard. Credit: Courtesy of Lukcia Sullivan

Shanna Saucier (left) watches as Lukcia Sullivan stirs bacon and wild mushroom risotto she was preparing for a five-course dinner party with her new friends. Credit: Linda Coan O'Kresik / BDN

At a dinner party in September, Lukcia meticulously dotted a ring of dill essential oil around plates containing chilled cucumber soup with jicama, watermelon and apples. She explained how the seasoning interacted with each ingredient to bring out the soup's zesty flavor.

Dressed in her fuchsia chef's coat, apron and cap, Lukcia held court for her guests, demonstrating how she simmered, boiled, braised, chopped, stewed and measured the ingredients to make gastronomical works of art like porchetta, roasted carrot soup and wild mushroom and bacon risotto.

After beginning her transition, Lukcia surrounded herself with a community of friends in their 20s, 30s and 40s. She often hosted people at her Hampden home, where she flexed the skills she picked up during a four-month stint at a southern Italian culinary school, freely pursuing a love of cooking that her father would once have forbidden.

Lukcia's embrace of gourmet cooking and new set of friends represented one dimension of her transition into the person she always knew herself to be.

Some friends found that, within Lukcia's story, they could see parts of their own. Shanna Saucier, 49, a frequent dinner party guest, met Lukcia at a bar in Bangor, shortly after Saucier separated from her husband. She was drawn to Lukcia's gregarious nature and a shared sense that the two women were at major crossroads in their lives.

Clockwise from top left: Lukcia Sullivan gives a helping hand to Jamie Jurgiewich (left), 21, with shredding a block of parmesan romano cheese at a dinner party Lukcia was hosting at her Hampden home in March. In early 2021, Lukcia attended the Italian Culinary Institute in Calabria, Italy and earned a certificate of Master of Italian Cuisine; Lukcia keeps an eye on the risotto while Madisyn Billings (left) and Jurgiewich help with preparations; Dolce prepared by Lukcia at her dinner party was a carrot cake with carrot sorbet served with a dessert wine; Lukcia enjoys a dinner party with the company of new friends at her home; Lukcia visits with her friends Jurgiewich (far

251

left) and Shanna Saucier at the dinner party. The photo in the background is from her five months at the institute. Credit: Linda Coan O'Kresik / BDN

"With my separation from my husband, I was finding my real self, and I was getting in touch with who Shanna really is," Saucier said. "So there might be some kind of parallel where Lukcia and I were both finally taking a stance and, regardless of the ramifications, we're just going to be who we are, who we need to be."

Jamie Jurgiewich, another friend and frequent dinner party guest, saw Lukcia as almost her grandmother. The two met last summer at a Veazie store where Jurgiewich worked at the time.

"I feel like she's going through some of the stages of being a girl that [I] went through or that maybe I'm currently going through," Jurgiewich, 21, said.

Others have been less accepting. Maine has some of the nation's strongest anti-discrimination laws, but that hasn't always reflected Lukcia's daily reality.

On one occasion, when Lukcia tried to strike up conversation with a woman at a bar, the woman's date posed a series of confrontational questions, pressing for intrusive details about her surgeries and why she transitioned at such a late age, Lukcia said.

Some people won't even sit near her. "I have people leave. They move one table away from me," Lukcia said. "People can deal with concepts, but it's difficult dealing with reality. I am reality."

Other times the repercussions are deeply personal. A man she went on a few dates with broke things off after his friends criticized him for seeing a transgender woman. And a number of Lukcia's relationships from earlier in life have also disappeared as she revealed more about her true identity.

But she never doubted her desire to transition.

"I just want to be a girl," Lukcia said. "That's all. I don't understand it. I just know I want it. And I've wanted it my whole life."

Since beginning her transition, Lukcia Sullivan has surrounded herself with new friends who are younger. Jamie Jurgiewich (left), 21, Lukcia and Shanna Saucier (right), 49, share a toast at a dinner party hosted by Lukcia at her home in Hampden. Credit: Linda Coan O'Kresik / BDN

Coming out

For a long time Lukcia wanted to talk about her inner struggle. She tried to come out several times over 25 years to her family members and former spouse, and she was laughed off. But her retirement marked a turning point. She finally had the time and money to pursue her dreams.

First came culinary school in southern Italy, in January 2020, which COVID cut short after a month. The following year, when she was allowed to return, she told the school that she had been presenting as a woman for three months, and would do so for the duration of the course and beyond. The institute accepted her with few questions.

It was one step to becoming more public about her identity.

She emerged from her training in April 2021 not only knowledgeable about charcuterie arrangements and how to cook gourmet seafood and pasta, but with a desire to let the world around her Hampden home know who she really was.

Most of her and her then-wife's friends and acquaintances did not know she had been presenting as a woman in her home since the previous fall, and it was time for them to know.

She put on her favorite matching pink blouse and skirt, and went to her butcher, pharmacist, the post office, grocery store and bike repair shop to reintroduce herself. Her transformation would not be complete without sharing it.

"I am Lukcia," she said.

Lukcia Sullivan enjoys her first outing to Mason's Brewing Company following her initial facial feminization surgery on Dec. 30, 2021. Lukcia met several of her new friends while eating there. After serving more than 20 years, Lukcia retired from the U.S. Army in 2004. She also served in the U.S. Coast Guard from January 1971 to December 1974. Credit: Linda Coan O'Kresik / BDN

Most accepted her right away. She attended her 50th high school class reunion later that summer, where everyone welcomed her as a transgender woman.

And she grew closer with Seymour, her sister, who visited last October. It was the first time they had seen each other in 12 years. Gone was the teenager Seymour remembered who effected macho behaviors to please their domineering father.

"I think we have a much better understanding of who we are," Seymour said. "I'm much happier with it."

At the same time, she worried for Lukcia's safety, **citing rising anti-transgender violence** and the current political climate.

"I want the world to be kind to her, but I think we want the world to be kind to anybody we love," Seymour said.

The two have since traveled back and forth between Maine and Georgia to visit each other.

In addition to two facial surgeries, Lukcia underwent a vaginoplasty in May, at the Papillon Gender Wellness Center in Pennsylvania. There, McGinn removed Lukcia's testicles and constructed a vagina using existing genital tissue. Lukcia described this latter procedure as the "completion" of her medical transition.

Lukcia in June. Credit: Linda Coan O'Kresik / BDN

Not all transgender people want or can afford the surgeries or hormonal treatments that Lukcia underwent. The three procedures, including associated travel and post-care expenses, like hired nurses, cost $143,000 out of pocket, which Lukcia paid using her savings and her military and USDA pensions.

Despite the financial cost, she compared the feeling after her first facial feminization surgery to floating on air.

"I already knew I was not going to turn back," she said. "But I still had to come up with the courage to follow through, to know that the decision for me was correct. It was the first step of taking myself seriously and believing in my dream."

Lukcia now dresses in the skirts she longed to wear for more than 60 years. She shrugs off the masculine mannerisms she struggled to parrot for decades. And she's preparing for a future that includes her chosen family of those who support her. One day, she hopes it will include a loving companion.

She is also speaking out, in a direct reversal from her youth and later adult years.

When Lukcia first awoke on that December afternoon after her first facial surgery, her head was wrapped in bandages, and she was unable to talk because of heavy medication. She offered her foot to visitors who couldn't touch her because of the risk of germs. She would spend her 69th birthday the following week at home, recovering.

She considered those minor inconveniences on a journey to embody the person she has always been.

"I laid down on that table. Then they strap you down to something that looks like a crucifix," she said. "Then they look at you and go, 'Are you ready?' And I looked up to them and went, 'I've been ready for so long.'"

I Will No Longer Edit Me

I sit and read every poem
The final proof before me
I sit as Lukcia almost four years now
Poems soon to be shared
I am so much stronger now than I was
Only every third or fourth poem
Makes me cry
I read my words and they ring so-so true
I can't believe I survived
Jennifer told me once...
"At some point it won't be special anymore,
You will just be a girl"
I hope that never comes true
Every morning, I wake up, and...
I can feel that I am a girl, and...
It feels great